Contents

Acknowledgements

The authors wish to thank all the students who gave us feedback to earlier drafts of this manuscript. We also would like to thank Joel Mendez, Isadora Rodriguez, and City University of New York (CUNY) faculty members for their input regarding the earlier drafts. Special thanks must go out to the students and colleagues who gave us permission to use their works in this textbook.

Introduction

There are many textbooks that discuss a single subject such as reading statistics, research methods, research writing, and writing topics such as paragraph development. This textbook is different. It gives students an overview of skills in research methods, statistics, and analyses of different types of assignments in classes, in addition to basic writing skills for students of all majors. For example, many students, regardless of their majors, do not have a solid background in the basic research concepts and they are lacking skills in writing. This is one of the main reasons they come to tutoring centers. Furthermore, professors do not have time to teach students the basic skills that they should have mastered in their previous introductory or foundation courses.

Rather than approaching its topics in a formulaic manner, this book outlines and discusses the most important concepts treated as the sole topic in many other texts. Essentially, it gives students a comprehensive background in the art and science of scientific research, as well as providing instruction on common writing assignment requirements encountered in research-based and general writing classes.

The practical approach to research-building and writing skills should allow this text to be well received by both first and second semester freshman, as well as more advanced students. This text is best used in conjunction with regularly assigned texts in order to supplement the most common assignments. All in all, this text is a reference guide for all college students.

Chapters 1 and 2 focus on study skills. These give the student the necessary basic skills to understand lectures, to learn vocabulary, read, and to take notes. This section concludes by discussing the different types of examinations and how to approach them. In part two, chapter 3 explains the different types of research, especially in the behavioral and social sciences. They also elaborate on how to read and interpret statistics. In the last section of this manual, Chapters 4 to 5 discuss plagiarism and the different types of assignments college students are expected to handle.

Overall, this textbook gives the student the essentials of research and writing that professors do not have time to review in their classes or that they assume students have mastered prior to advanced-level courses. Instructors assume that once introductory or foundation courses are taken, students are able to apply them to their other classes. This supplementary textbook is essential for any undergraduate or graduate student, who desires a better understanding of necessary college assignments and skills.

All students would benefit from this manual. Freshman and sophomores would benefit from the section on study skills, which include listening to lectures, taking notes, and studying for examinations. Lectures are sometimes difficult to follow. This text explains the different patterns that instructors use to give lectures. It also gives tips on how to take notes and how to study for examinations. Study skills are the most important tools that must be mastered to succeed in college.

Also, all undergraduate and graduate students would well receive the part of the manual discussing typical assignments. They are broken down in different ways. They are first defined so that the student knows what is being asked of him or her. Then, instructions are given on how to tackle the assignments step by step. Tips for time and task management are also included, so students can maximize their efforts.

Furthermore, the chapters that talk about research concepts, writing, and how to read research would be especially useful to science-oriented students, as well as graduate students. These sections give the student an overview of reading and writing research. This facilitates their understanding when they read journal articles and scientific texts. Students will become faster and more efficient as they develop these skills.

Since every student is different in their understanding and mastery of the concepts included in this text, it is designed to be a reference at all levels of a student's college career. Each student will find that he or she will use different sections of it during different times in his or her academic career. Essentially, this textbook gives the student a foundation for studying, conducting research, and for completing common assignments in classes.

PART 1: BASIC COLLEGE LEARNING SKILLS

CHAPTER 1

STUDY SKILLS

Setting Goals

The goal of most college students is to get a college degree with the intention of getting a good-paying job. Many students set goals for themselves, but they do not carry them out. It is not easy to juggle school, work, and family and personal time.

Setting goals involves prioritizing them so they can be accomplished in a reasonable period of time. Certain things must come before other things. For example, when setting a study schedule, the tests and homework that is due immediately should be completed before the things that are due later on. The best way to do organize one's workload is to make a *schedule*. The student needs to allocate time for work, study, and personal time. By making a schedule, one is more likely to stick to it. Figure 1 shows an example of a schedule that he or she might have.

Looking at Figure 1.1, this student is balancing his or her work, class, study, and family, and exercise. It is important that the student lets his or her family members the change from the everyday routine before school starts. This will limit the frustrations the other family members may have with the schedule change. It will also create better interpersonal relationships at home. By not preparing family members for a change in schedule, problems at home can lead to future academic problems. This can prevent a student from graduating. For the interest of every family member, it is best to let all family members know what is going to be the change in routine and what will be expected, so everyone will get along and the student can attend college with few frustrations and problems at home.

Figure 1.1: Daily Schedule for Fall 2005 Semester

	Monday	Tuesday	Wednesday	Thursday	Friday
9am	Bring kids to baby sitter	Work	Bring kids to baby sitter	Work	Bring kids to baby sitter
10am	Biology 181	Work	Biology 181	Work	Study
11am	Biology 181	Work	Biology 181	Work	Study
12pm	Biology 181	Work	Biology 181	Work	Work
1pm	Lunch	Work	Lunch	Work	Work
2pm	Study	Work	Study	Work	Work
3pm	Study	Work	Study	Work	Work
4pm	Chemistry 166	Study	Chemistry 166	Study	Work
5pm	Chemistry 166	Study	Chemistry 166	Study	Exercise
6pm	Exercise	Study	Exercise	Study	Pick kids up from baby sitter
7pm	Pick kids up from baby sitter	Study	Pick kids up from baby sitter	Study	Family time
8pm	Family time	Family time	Family time	Family time	Family time
9pm	Family time	Family time	Family time	Family time	Family time
10pm	Study	Family time	Study	Family time	Family time
11pm	Study	Bed	Study	Bed	Bed

Vocabulary Learning

Vocabulary is best learned by learning the *affixes* (prefixes, roots, and suffixes) of words. *Prefixes* are parts of words that come before the base. The *base* is also called the *root* or the *stem*. The base is the main part of a word. A *suffix* is the part of word that comes after the base. Once the affixes are learned, they are the same for every word. As one looks for the word parts, he or she is breaking down a word. This makes it easier to guess the meaning of a particular word if it is foreign to the student.

If we look at the word *prediction* (see Figure 1.2), it can be broken down into its parts. This word comes from Latin word parts. Most words in English have their roots in Latin or Greek. If students take the time to learn these affixes, they will have an easier time with learning vocabulary. This last statement is especially true in the sciences.

Figure 1.2: Affixes

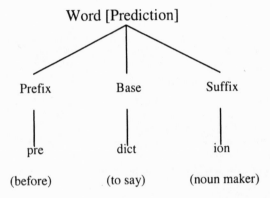

There are some inexpensive books that approach learning vocabulary in this format:

    (i) 30 *Days to a More Powerful Vocabulary* by Dr. William Funk and Norman Lewis;

    (ii) *Instant Word Power* by Norman Lewis;

    (iii) *Word Power Made Easy* by Norman Lewis;

    (iv) *English Words from Latin and Greek Elements* by Donald Ayers; and

    (v) *NTC's Dictionary of Greek and Latin Origins*

College Lectures

The college lecture is one of the main ways students are exposed to content material in higher education. In most college lectures, students have to listen to a professor speak for long periods of time while taking notes (Lively, Pisoni, van Summers, & Bernacki, 1993). This process is not as easy as it seems: (a) listening; (b) selecting; (c) summarizing; and (d) writing (Koren, 1997). This multitasking makes it one of the most difficult things to do in college. Let us address each part separately in order to facilitate the process.

Listening, in terms of a college lecture, involves hearing what sentences the instructor is saying (also called *utterances*) while, at the same time, trying to understand the utterances. While listening to a college lecture, one must look for several things: (a) the pattern of the lecture; (b) key words or phrases that are repeated; and (c) anything a professor states that is important or will be on an examination.

The pattern of a lecture is very important for following and anticipating what comes next. Despite the lecture styles, they all have the same elements. The only difference is how they are being presented. Three lecture styles are discussed in this chapter.

One style is a definition with the target word plus a restatement (Fahmay, Jackson, & Bilton, 1990). The *target word* is the word being defined. A *restatement* is a restatement of something in different words. An example of this is:

John, a compound bilingual is someone who learned two languages at the same time.

In this case, this is an explanation of a concept that was previously mentioned. The base word is *compound bilingual* and the reformulation is *someone who learned two languages at the same time.*

Another style is where the target word is followed by two restatements. An example of this is:

Some people are shy... in other words, diffident or timid.

Here, *shy* is the base word. *Diffident or timid* are reformulations.

The third style that is discussed in this chapter is a target word proceeded by a repetition and by a restatement. Here is an example of this style:

This is an example of cleft palate ... cleft palate which is when the palatine bones don't fuse together at 3 months.

The base word is *cleft palate*, and *when the palatine bones don't fuse together* is the reformulation.

Selecting means picking out what information is important. One way to pick the key points out is to look for cues. A cue can be a phrase such as "You will need to know this" (Scerbo et al., 1992). Another cue is intonation. Intonation refers to the stress the instructor gives to words when he or she speaks. For example, if the stress is on the last part of an utterance, then it is a question (Selkirk, 1995). Besides cues, repetition of a word(s) is a way to pick the important things out of a lecture.

A **summary** is a brief synopsis of something. After determining if the utterance is important, the student has to summarize it in his or her own words if possible.

The final step in the process is to **write** the utterance down in the notebook or whatever one writes notes in. What the student writes down in class while listening to a college lecture is called *class or lecture notes*. Class notes should be brief for three reasons:

1. The student should have already read the material before going to class. Therefore, the material should not be completely new. (This assumes that the student has been given the material to read beforehand.)

2. It is more important for the student to listen than take very detailed class notes. Only words and phrases, and anything that is emphasized in class should be written in class notes because most everything else is in the handouts or in the textbooks.
3. A student cannot focus on two things at the same time. Meaning, one cannot give his or her full attention to what a professor is saying while writing down class notes.

Listening to a lecture and taking class notes is a very difficult task. If a student adheres to the above tips, he or she will have an easier time comprehending the material discussed in class.

Studying for Examinations

Studying is a time-consuming process that can be facilitated by a few easy steps. **Study notes** are notes that a student uses to study for examinations. They include class notes (as discussed above) and *book notes* (notes from the textbook and other materials). One of the recommended ways to make study notes is to type or rewrite them into a word processor such as Word or Word Perfect; they can also be recorded on to an audio CD.

They should be reviewed two to three times a week. This will reduce the time spent studying for a test when it gets closer to the examination; in other words, cramming for an examination will not be necessary if one studies this way. Studying should begin from the first day of class. It is recommended that the notes be typed or rewritten within 24 hours of the lecture because, after 24 hours, the student is most likely to forget the information. If the student cannot do it within 24 hours after the class, it should be done as soon as possible. Some students make the mistake and over study. Over studying can hurt one's chances of doing well on an examination. By over studying, the mind cannot rest. It is like a muscle like any other muscle in the body.

Types of Examinations

Many students do not have strategies to take tests. When things go awry, students panic and make hasty decisions. When one is taking a test, it is recommended that he or she completes the questions that can be answered automatically first. The consequence of not doing it this way is that the student will remain on a particular question and not progress. This could cause him or her not to finish a test in the allotted time.

When taking **Multiple Choice M/C tests**, the best approach is process of elimination. The student should eliminate the answers that are definitely wrong to increase the chances of an educated guess if the answer is not clear. Also, one should answer the questions that can be completed automatically first. After all, a 50 percent chance is better than a 25 percent chance of getting a problem correct.

Short answer tests are not essay examinations. They do not require an introduction, body, and conclusion. All that is required is to answer the question with just the information that is being requested. Many students try to add additional information that is unnecessary. This unnecessary information can hurt one's grade, especially if it is incorrect or not pertinent to the question.

Essay examinations are very stressful for students. A professor is not looking for a perfect paper. What he or she is looking for is an edited first draft. This means that the essay should be written in Standard American English and be edited. Since this type of examination is done within a limited time frame, an instructor cannot hold the student to the same expectations as an essay that a student has been given well in advance. In most cases, the questions will be about applying concepts to their applications.

Open-book examinations are not intended to be easy. For these tests, a professor may allow his or her students to use their books and/or their class notes during test time. This can be for whole examination or just for a certain part of it.

Take-home examinations are not intended to be easy like open-book examinations. These tests are graded with to the highest standards since a student has access to all the materials when working on it. These examinations can be a series of short answer questions and/or essays, which can be answered separately or in the form of an essay, or one essay question in most cases.

CHAPTER 2

READING DIFFERENT ACADEMIC TEXTS

How to Read

Reading is a process that requires one to do many things at the same time. The reader has to be *interacting with the text*. In other words, he or she must be able to predict what will come next immediately after each section by asking oneself the *wh-questions* (who, what, where, when, why, and how) while reading the text.

How to Read General Academic Texts

Reading academic texts such as textbooks and essays is not easy to do. Many times, the texts are very technical. For this reason, they turn off many students. Why? Students have to reread them many times, which makes them frustrated. This chapter will help students read faster and more efficient.

What makes an efficient reader? An efficient reader is a person who finds the thesis statement first. A *thesis statement* is a statement that expresses what the whole text will be about. It is usually found in the conclusion. However, it can be solely in the introduction, or it can be in the conclusion and introduction. Next, the headings are read. Then, he or she outlines the text. Lastly, the body is read. In other words, a good reader reads backwards. On the contrary, a non-efficient reader will read a text like a romance novel. This means that he or she reads from page one to page xxx.

The efficient reader or writer is predicting what will come next. In other words, efficient readers put themselves as writers when they read, just as efficient writers put themselves as readers when the write. Knowledge of how a text is a written facilitates how to read the text at hand. There are three parts to any written text: introduction, body, and conclusion. The introduction may or may not contain the thesis statement, but it must introduce the *topic* or *theme*. The body is where all the supporting reasons and details are included. The conclusion is where the writer must restate the thesis statement and briefly mention what was discussed in the body of the text.

The most efficient method of reading an academic text is *prediction*. This means that the reader will predict what each section of text will be about before actually reading it. In order to predict, one has to have a general sense of what the text is about. Following a series of steps does this. It can be thought of as baking a cake. The baker mixes all the dry ingredients together and all the wet ingredients together before putting them together in the mixer. Reading is no different.

Here is the order how one should read an academic text. The *first step* is to read the title and predict what the text will be about. It should be noted that most titles tell what the text is about. A title does not have to tell what a text will be about.

Step two is to read the conclusion. The purpose of a conclusion is to summarize the text. A conclusion can also give further recommendations for research or give the reader the author's opinion(s) about the subject. How does one know where the conclusion begins? Finding the conclusion can be a little difficult. The easiest way to locate it is to go to the end of the text and see where it starts becoming general. Where it becomes general, write the word *conclusion* above that paragraph if it is not done already. In other words, you will make a subheading.

Step three is to read the *introduction*. An introduction is the part of the text that introduces what it will be about. It is very general. The goal here is to find where the introduction ends. How does one know where the introduction ends? The introduction ends where the text starts becoming specific. Write the word *body* in the margins where the introduction ends.

Step four is to read the subheadings. These *subheadings* are used to divide by the body into subsections. These subsections are like texts inside of texts. They are like papers inside of papers. Each subsection has an introduction, body, and conclusion.

Up to this point, the reader has found the thesis statement and has created an outline of the text. This is what we call *part one of reading*. Part one of reading, is creating an outline of the text. By creating an outline of the text, the reader knows what the thesis statement is and has a gist of what is inside the body of the text. All that is left is to read the body of the text. This is *part two of reading*. In other words, the reader is going to fill in the outline he or she has created (see Figure 2.1).

Figure 2.1: Framework for Reading Academic Text

Steps in order of how to read academic texts:
1. Title
2. Conclusion
3. Introduction
4. Headings and sub-headings
5. Body of the text

To review, reading involves two parts. The first part is to do is to determine what type of text it is. There are many types of texts: argumentative, descriptive, persuasive, comparison and contrast, and process. The only way this can be determined is by reading the thesis statement and making an outline of the text, which is discussed above.

The second part is to find what is the writer's pattern and fill in the outline created in part one. This makes it easier for the reader to follow the text. Once the type of text is confirmed, the reader needs to find a pattern that is present throughout the entire piece of writing. Each writer has his or her own style. This is the part two of reading.

What has just been described above is for any general academic text. When referring to specific academic texts (see next section), the same rules apply. The only difference is that the reader has to apply this to the format of whatever he or she is reading. Once a student knows the basics of reading, the only thing that is has to be done is apply it to the specific format. The rest is the same.

Reading a Journal Article

Keeping in mind what was said about a general academic text is the basic principle for reading a journal article. When many students are confronted with the task of reading a journal article, their hearts start beating faster and their fear begins to take over. Part of their problem is that they do not understand the basic concepts in research. Another problem is that many students do not know the correct order that each section should be read in and how to read each one. This chapter will focus on how to read a journal article.

Let us start with the first problem mentioned above. If one does not have an understanding of basic research, then the student will have a difficult time in picking out things such as the different variables, which will be discussed in Chapter 3.

Format for an Experimental, Quasi-Experimental, and Qualitative Journal Article

The **abstract** is the first part of a journal article. This is a brief summary of the article in 120 words or less unless specified by the journal editors. It is written in the same order as the sections of a journal article are in most cases. The first part is the purpose of the study, commonly called the purpose and problem statement. In general academic texts, this is called the thesis statement or thesis. The method of the study comes next. This is followed by the results. Finally, the conclusions of the study, called the Discussion, are the last thing to be mentioned.

The **introduction** is next. This is similar to an academic essay. The thesis statement, more specifically called the purpose or problem statement is usually found in the conclusion of the introduction. The first part of an introduction is previous studies, the literature review. Then, a summary of the previous studies follows. Finally, the purpose and problem statement, any research questions, and why the study was conducted will conclude the introduction.

The **methods** section is next. This section describes the procedures of how the subjects, or *participants*, were selected. The *procedures* (tests and tasks) for how the study was conducted come next. Here, identifying the variables are extremely important in making sense of what the stimuli will be for the tests. The independent, dependent, and control variables are the most common ones. These variables determine the groups, control or experimental, and who gets a certain stimuli. This part also includes any tests the participants will perform in detail. The last part to this section is the analysis of the data. The researcher(s) explain how the data will be analyzed.

The **results** are the findings or results. This is where all of the scores from the tests performed are reported. In other words, only the facts or what was found is in this section; as the saying goes, "Just the facts, Ma'am."

The **discussion** is the interpretations of the findings. In this section, the purpose and problem statement is restated. Then, the principal results are stated, interpreted and compared with previous studies. Any limitations or biases are also discussed. Finally, recommendations for future research are discussed.

The **references** are the body of literature that the investigator(s) used in the introduction for previous studies and comparing their results with the previous studies.

The **appendices** are used to show any lists of words or questions that may important or interesting for the reader to know (see Figure 2.2).

Figure 2.2: Procedures for Reading Mixed methods Articles

Steps in order of how to read quantitative, qualitative, and mixed methods journal articles:
1. Title
2. Abstract
3. Discussion
4. Introduction
   a. Start with the conclusion then go to introduction
5. Headings and subheadings
6. Body of the journal article

Format for a Theory, Practice Oriented, and Literature Review Journal Articles

The **abstract** is the first part of a journal article. This is a brief summary of the article in 120 words or less unless specified by the journal editors. It is written in the same order as the sections of a journal article are in most cases. The first part is the purpose of the study, commonly called the purpose and problem statement. The studies come next. This is followed by the interpretation of the studies.

The **introduction** is next. This is similar to an academic essay. The thesis statement, or the purpose of the study, is usually found in the conclusion of the introduction. The first part of an introduction is previous studies. Then, a summary of the previous studies follows. Finally, the purpose and problem statement and any research questions will conclude the introduction.

The section which describes what studies will be discussed according to the subjects, or participants, how the procedures for each study, and their results for review of the literature articles, is the **Themes from Studies.** For theory articles, this section explains **how the particular theory works**.

The **discussion** is the interpretations of the findings of the different studies. In this section, the principal results of the major studies elaborated on are interpreted and reviewed in the context of the purpose and problem statement. Fi-

Reading Different Academic Texts

nally, recommendations for future research are discussed. The **references** are the body of literature that the investigator(s) use in the study.

Reading an academic text is not easy. There is a lot of information that a student has to decipher. How it is done depends what kind of text it is. If the student follows what has been stated above, he or she will have an easier time.

PART II: RESEARCH AND DATA ESTIMATION

CHAPTER 3

Research and Data Estimation

Research is a systematic investigation to establish a principle or fact. The process of establishing a principle or fact is referred to as a methodology (scientific method) and is normally made with some assumptions. The process starts with the determination of a sample size and the collection of data to evaluate a theory. The data is then estimated with an important objective of testing a hypothesis for validity or spuriousness to make inferences.

Data Analysis

The selection of a research topic is only the beginning of an unsettling process, which includes analyzing and estimating data, and making inferences from the estimation. *Data analysis* is defined here to mean the application of statistical and logical techniques to describe, summarize, and compare data. Once data is obtained, it has to be estimated and evaluated to arrive at a meaningful theoretical conclusion. The theoretical aspect is directly related to a thesis statement, which must then be evaluated, to be accepted or rejected through hypothesis testing.

Data are information that comes from observations, counts, and responses. They could be either plentiful or scarce. They should, however, be sought and received with great caution. The caution is essential to maintain the integrity of the research motive. Bad data generate bad results and defeats the purpose of the research endeavor. The researcher is consequently obligated to check the source and quality of the data before proceeding with his analysis.

Data could be numerical (in the form of real numbers—1, 2, 3, -1, -2...) or categorical (in the form of characteristics—male, female, black, white, Hispanic...). For the sake of numerical estimation, categorical variables could be given numerical values, for example, 1 for black and 0 for white. When such a transformation is made, the variable is said to be a dummy. Hence, the phrase "dummy variables". Variables are measurable characteristics, which take varying values. For example, labor input is a variable if an employer can vary the number of people hired: 200, 300, or even 1000 over time. The opposite of a variable is a constant. A constant does not change; therefore, the change of a constant is always zero.

Data may also be analyzed from three perspectives: (i) time series; (ii) cross-section; and (iii) pooled. Time series data show a chronological sequence of observations on a particular variable, meaning the change of a particular variable over time. Time series data may be compiled daily, monthly, quarterly, or annually.

Cross-section data are collected on one or more variables at the same point in time. As such, they are data on many units, such as individuals, households, firms, governments, or countries at the same time. They are otherwise known as parallel data. A familiar problem with cross-section data is heterogeneity or differences in units and variances. As a factual matter, some nations or firms are big, and others small; some are wealthier, and others are poorer; some nations are densely populated and others are relatively sparsely populated.

Pooled data combine the elements of time series and cross-section data. A special type of pooled data is the longitudinal or micropanel data, which is also known as "panel data". In panel data, the same cross-sectional unit is surveyed over time. Table 3.1 summarizes the categories of data.

Table 3.1: Types of Data

Time Series		Cross-Section /Pooled		Panel		
Year	NYSE (Avg. Daily Trade Volume $)	Minimum wage (2000/5)		Mortgage Backed Securities Issuances ($ Billions)		
1999	809M	Alaska	$7.15	Fannie Mae	1999	270
2000	1042M	Washington	$7.16		2000	179
2001	1240M	Oregon	$7.05		2001	483
2002	1441M	Georgia	$5.15	Freddie Mac	1999	216
2003	1398M	New York	$5.15		2000	139
2004	1442M	Texas	$5.15		2001	254

In close association with the quality of data is the sample size. To understand the concept of sample size, the researcher might want to imagine how much information is essential to draw a convincing conclusion. The whole idea of undertaking a research experiment revolves around obtaining a result that would meaningfully help to evaluate a theory, arrive at a principle, corroborate a fact, or generate profit. The sample on which the research is based must, therefore, provide convincing conclusions.

Invariably, the availability of data would more often than not impinge, or have an effect on the determination of a sample size. This makes the preview of data availability an equally serious matter as developing a hypothesis. It would be meaningless to have a very nice and erudite hypothesis, for which there is no data. Simply put, the hypothesis could not be evaluated or tested. Presenting a topic for a research investigation, without exploring the possibilities of obtaining the required data, may result in the premature abandonment of a topic. It is important to note that exploring the possibilities of data availability is not synonymous with data mining. Premature withdrawal from a topic might give the appearance of inadequate preparation or indecisiveness. This might also be a first cause of frustration with the research process.

A sample is a subset of a population. Population refers to the complete set of objects of interest. In theory, it is the collection of all outcomes, responses, measurements, or counts that are of interest to the researcher. It is, by definition, unobtainable because generally researchers are not able to access all the objects of interest. For example, suppose a researcher is interested in knowing whether colleges which use Dell computers have a high graduation rate. It is apparent that the researcher would neither be able to know all the colleges using Dell computers (the population), nor obtain data on all the colleges using Dell computers. He is, therefore, confronted with a dilemma of how best to obtain information (data) that would approximate the population which he is trying to estimate.

The first inclination might be a problematic one, using counts (colleges) of a population that are readily available without including those which are not readily available. This type of sampling, which is generally considered a sample of convenience, is critically inadequate and is likely to produce unreliable results because of the exclusion of other relevant parts of the population.

It is generally preferable to take a random sample. Apart from the random sample, other methods could be classified as systematic, clustered, or stratified. These alternative options must be used with some amount of precaution, as they typically exhibit flaws of their own, especially lack of variation if the sample is arranged and the variables are categorical.

A systematic sample is one for which a sub/sample is selected from a grand sample (a population) by selecting the kth subject/observation from the grand sample. To determine the sub-sample size, the researcher must determine the kth subject/observation to be included in his sub/sample. The grand sample to kth-observation ratio ultimately determines the sample size. For example, a grand sample size of 800 from which every 20th observation is to be included will yield a sub-sample of 800/20 or 40. Alternatively, a sub-sample to grand-sample ratio of 1/8 (assuming a sub/sample size of 100 is desired) would indicate that the starting point must be from the eighth observation and systematically in that sequence going forward. Subjectivity bias is largely contingent on the type of variable investigated and pre-sampling considerations or foreknowledge of the grand sample. A cluster sample is similar to a systematic sample in so far as they are both sub-samples and nothing more in terms of fundamental idea.

A cluster sample is a sample derived from clusters or groups. A population is divided into groups/clusters. This form of sampling is normally deemed to be desirable when a geographical population is scattered and it becomes impractical to be able to reach individuals of a population. For example, the population of a town could be divided into households, which consist of individuals. From the households, a sample could be drawn to reflect individual characteristics. This is generally known as the "random sampling of clusters."

The collection of data based on a stratified sample involves the division of the sample into strata because of a common characteristic, which might be the result of socio-economic or income differentials. In this case, each segment of a population is represented. The idea of inclusion makes stratified samples more attractive than simple random samples when status, race, age, gender, religious, and/or political ideologies are involved.

There are good statistical or econometric reasons for the sample size to be large. Apart from targeting the elusive population, there has to be an element of randomness so that the sample is not biased. For example, if a researcher wants to know whether an increase in advertising increases the sale of bench pressers, he is likely to get a much more accurate result if he chooses a sample that includes males and females, young and old, rich and poor and slim and obese. Choosing a sample of a collection of slim teenagers who are fond of bench pressing would yield a biased and deceptive result. Drawing conclusions from such a sample and making policies based on such a sample would be dangerously misleading, and it might detrimentally increase the cost of marketing, and reduce profits.

The option to use a sample is based on a probability distribution, which is generally tied to a *Law of Averages*. The *Law of Averages* states that the average of independent observations of random variables with the same probability distribution is increasingly likely to be closest to the expected value of the random variables as the number of observations (samples) increases.

By relating samples to probability, two concepts are important: (i) the average of independent observations of random variables; and (ii) a normal distribution. A *variable* is defined as random when its value is randomly chosen from a population or when its value is subject to random variation. The average, which is also known as the mean, is a measure of location. The average could take the form of an arithmetic mean, a weighted mean, or a geometric mean. It is the central value around which the values of a data would cluster. The researcher would, therefore, like his observations to be as close to the value of the expected mean as possible.

The Average/Mean

The average is a measure of central tendency and a powerful piece of information to determine how close or far away other values are situated from it. Other measures of central tendency are the median (the middle data entry of a well ordered or sequentially ordered data) and the mode (the entry with the most frequency). Knowledge of the average facilitates three important measures of variation: (i) mean absolute deviation (MAD); (ii) variance; and (iii) standard deviation.

Knowledge of the average enables the development of a Central Limit Theorem (CLT), which holds that averaging almost always leads to a bell-shaped distribution for which the majority of the values of the data would be clustered around the mean while the minority would taper off away from the mean with the tails of the bell-shaped curve asymptotically reaching zero. This is a powerful theory which allows for standardization around a mean.

The mean (arithmetic) of a data is the sum of data entries divided by the number of entries or observations. The Greek Mu (μ) is normally used to denote the population mean, while x bar ($\overline{x}$) is normally used to denote the sample mean. In complete form, the population mean is defined as: $\mu = (\sum X)/n$; and the sample mean as: $\overline{x} = (\sum X)/n$, where $\sum X$ is the sum or total of data entries, and n is the number of entries. For example, suppose we want to determine the average price of dress shirts and we take a small sample of 16 brands for dollar ($) prices as shown in Table 5.2.

At the end of our primary task when we total the prices of shirts for the various brands, we would realize that the total cost is $451.84. To get the average cost, we will then need to divide our total cost by the number of brands (16) we have selected for our sample. The number of brands is otherwise known as the number of entries or observations. Our average for this sample will then be: 451.84/16 = 28.24. We could then conclude that the average cost of dress shirts based on our limited sample is $28.24.

This data on the prices of dress shirts offer other information. Looking at the data in its ordered form, we could tell the median and the mode. The median is the middle data entry. Because the data has an even number of entries (16), we cannot decisively apportion the data into two equal halves. We must, therefore, average out the two middle data entries to get the median. This turns out to be $27.99, which is also pretty close to the arithmetic mean ($28.24) in this case. Just by looking at the data, we could also see that $31.99 occurred more frequently than any other price. Since $31.99 has the greatest frequency, it is the mode of the data. If $26.99 had occurred as many times as $31.99, the data would have been bimodal. If the sample were large enough and symmetrical, the mean would be identical to the mode and median.

There are other forms of averages which are worth noting. These include the weighted mean/average and the geometric mean/average. A *weighted mean* is a mean which is the result of the attachment of weights to data entries or observations. It is conventional for the attached weights to average out to 1. Weights are normally assigned when some entries or scores carry more significance or importance than others. For example, a Statistics exam might be more important than a Gym exam to get admission into a graduate school, but the Gym exam might be more important than a writing exam. We could assign the following weights: 5, 4, and 1, if we think that the Gym exam is four times more important than the writing exam, but that the Statistics exam is five times more important than the writing exam to get admission into graduate school. Given the weights, suppose one scores 70 in Statistics, 80 in Gym, and 90 in Writing. The weighted average of theses courses in terms of their importance or significance becomes:

$$[70*5 + 80*4 + 90*1]/10 = 76\%.$$

Table 3.2: Dress Shirt Prices

Dress Shirt	Price ($)
Izod Poplin	22.99
Arrow Dover	22.99
Tab Collar	24.99
Van Heusen	24.99
Arrow	24.99
Calvin Klein	26.99
Paul Frederick	26.99
Jos. A Bank	**26.99**
Palm Beach	**28.99**
Port Authority	28.99
Perry Ellis	31.99
Tommy Hilfiger	31.99
Eddie Bauer	31.99
Polo	31.99
Nordstrom	31.99
Geoffrey Beene	31.99
Total/$\sum$	**451.84**

Notice that without the weights, the arithmetic mean would have been higher (80%). The weighted average is low in this case because the subject with the most weight got the lowest score, and the subject with the least weight got the highest score. The weighted mean could be represented in mathematical notation as follows:

$$w_m = [x_1w_1 + x_2w_2 + x_3w_3 \ldots + x_nw_n] / [w_1 + w_2 + w_3 \ldots + w_n];$$

where w_m = weighted average; w = assigned weights; and x = real numerical values.

The geometric mean (gm) of a set of n numbers is the nth root of the product of the numbers. For example, suppose we reduce our shirt sample to the first three brands and we are interested in taking the geometric mean of the three brands.

Table 3.3: Geometric Mean

Shirt	Price ($)
Izod Poplin	22.99
Arrow Dover	22.99
Tab Collar	24.99

$$gm = 3\sqrt{22.99*22.99*24.99} = (22.99*22.99*24.99)^{1/3}$$
$$gm = 23.63$$

The geometric mean is normally useful to calculate the concentration of data with extreme values, and for calculating the average rate of change per period of time for quantities, which grow over time. An example of this is the average rate of return on an investment.

Frequency

The frequency with which observations occur in a data could be arranged and graphed. For example, suppose we want to find the ages of males attending college. We hypothetically interview 1000 honest male students who correctly report their ages. If 500 of the 1000 students tell us that their ages range from 20-30 years, the frequency for ages 20-30 becomes 500. Frequency distribution is normally provided in a table of classes or intervals of data entries. Table 3.4 exemplifies the analysis. Of the one thousand respondents, four hundred are between the ages of 30 and 40 years; and one hundred are between 50 and 60 years.

Table 3.4: A Frequency Table

Ages of College Students	Frequency (number of data value obtained)
20-30 years	500
30-40 years	400
50-60 years	100
Total	1000

A *class width or size* is the difference between the lower and upper class boundaries. In the above example, there are 3 classes; each with boundaries: (i) 20-30; (ii) 30-40; and (iii) 50-60. For the first class, the lower limit is 20 and the upper limit is 30. Given the boundaries/limits of a particular class, a class mid-point/mark could be calculated. For example, the mark of the first class is:

$$[20 + 30]/2 = 25.$$

Values of a frequency table can also be used to calculate the relative fre-quency. The *relative frequency* is found by dividing the frequency of a class by the total measurement or frequency. Suppose we want to find the relative fre-quency of occurrences between the ages of 20-30 years from Table 3.4. We can do so by dividing the frequency of that class (500) by the total amount of fre-quencies (1000); 500/1000 = 0.5. The values of Table 3.4 could then enable us to construct a table with relative frequency distribution as shown in Table 3.5.

Notice that the relative frequency adds up to one. Relative frequency must always add up to one, which in percentage form is equivalent to an aggregate of 100% for a cumulative sample of cases. Relative frequency distribution can be depicted graphically in the form of a frequency histogram; where a frequency histogram is a set of rectangles in a Cartesian coordinate system. The line con-necting the midpoints of the tops of the rectangles of the histogram is known as the frequency polygon, which is illustrated in Figure 3.1. Notice that the relative frequency is on the *y*-axis and that the measurements are on the *x*-axis. The rela-tive frequency must always be on the *y*-axis.

Table 3.5: A Frequency and Relative Frequency Table

Ages of College Students	Frequency (number of data value obtained)	Relative frequency
20-30 years	500	0.5
30-40 years	400	0.4
50-60 years	100	0.1
Total	1000 (cumulative)	1.0

Figure 3.1: A Relative Frequency and Frequency Polygon

Relative Frequency (ages)

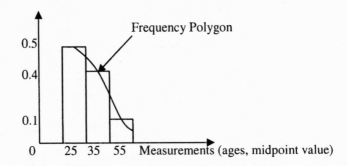

Apart from using the mean and the frequency or mode to show the concentration or spread of data, a box-and-whisker plot could be used to show in pictorial form how dispersed the values of a data set are around the median.

Box-and-whisker Plot

The construction of a box-and-whisker plot is pretty straightforward once a basic understanding of the median is obtained. The values of the data must first be arranged in ordered or sequential form (i.e., ascending order). For example, suppose the final examination scores of 15 Statistics students are those recorded in Table 3.6. How could a box-and-whisker plot be used to show the spread around the median?

The initial challenge is to divide the data into equal parts (fractiles). The median divides data into two equal parts. The two equal parts could further be divided into four equal parts to obtain quartiles, meaning that the values of the data could be partitioned into four parts using three quartiles. The median is, therefore, the second quartile and the difference between the third and first quartiles is the interquartile range (IQR). The box is made up of the values of the three quartiles, and the horizontal lines connecting the lowest and highest values of the data to the box are known as the "whiskers".

After the data have been arranged in sequence, a number line could be used to map out the values of the data to obtain the relevant quartiles that are necessary to construct the box-and-whisker plot.

To do the box-whisker plot we first organize the data of Statistics scores in ascending order. The data would, therefore, take the ordered form shown in Figure 3.2.

Table 3.6: Statistics Examination Scores for 15 Students

Name	Score
Jane	50
Dexter	80
Jasmine	70
Luisa	82
Peter	90
Christopher	95
James	60
Andrew	40
Elaine	66
John	88
George	75
Frank	81
Rosalina	55
Angelina	98
Robert	63

Figure 3.2: Box-whisker Plot of Statistics Scores

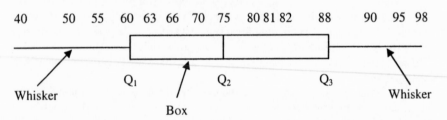

The median score of the data is 75. There is no need to take the average of 70 and 75 or 75 and 80 to get the median in this case because we have an odd number of observations (15). Even number of observations would require taking the average of the two numbers in the middle of the data set to get the median.

Since 75 is the median score, the upper value scores would range from 80 to 98, while the lower value scores would range from 40 to 70. The score which divides the lower value scores into two is 60 (which is the first quartile, and the score which divides the upper value scores into two is 88 (which is the third quartile). These quartiles constitute the box which shows the spread of the Statistics Scores around the median value and the IQR is 28. The whiskers show the range of the lowest and highest scores.

So far our analysis of data has focused on *central tendency*: the tendency of data to cluster around a central value, be it the mean, the mode, or the median. The closeness of values around the central value is usually estimated by the standard deviation or variance, in particular to compare the spread of clustered or group observations, or changes in a clustered trend, the greater the standard deviation and the greater the dispersion.

Variation/Variance and Standard Deviation

Variation is traditionally calculated in terms of distance from the mean/average, and this method is used normally in place of the range which takes only two values into consideration. Table 3.7 shows per capita egg consumption in countries which have been selected from data compiled by the International Egg Commission. The sample size (33) has been deliberately selected to accommodate the arguments of the CLT. This theorem will be discussed in depth later. Suffice it to say for now that this sample size would enable a researcher to assume that his/her sample has a normal distribution (i.e.) enough information to make comparisons with what could be expected if he/she could observe an entire population of events or occurrences, which is highly improbable.

There are two important measures of variation: the variance which is calculated from the Mean Absolute Deviation (MAD); and the standard deviation, which is calculated from the variance. Though these concepts might sound convoluted, there are intuitive ways of understanding them. Deviation ordinarily means to stray or wander away. The question then becomes from what? In Statistics or Econometrics, deviation is normally measured as a distance away from the mean or average.

Alluding to the per capita egg consumption in Table 3.7 is a practical way of dealing with the concept. We might want to know, for example, by how much the consumption of eggs per person in the US or Spain is different from the average consumption of eggs per person in the rest of the world. Alternatively, when the average per capita consumption is almost identical, the standard deviation would give an idea as to how dispersed the amount of per capita consumption is (about the mean) when countries are compared.

If we take a look at Table 5.7 we will realize that the total or sum of deviations from the mean, $\sum(x-\mu)$ is 0. This is always true, because the positive deviations from the mean cancel out the negative ones. The mean does not help us very much to explain everything that we might want to know about per capita egg consumption in the US. For example, we might want to know something about per capita consumption of eggs in the US in relation to the rest of the world, without focusing only on the sample at hand. To do that, we would want to know the standard deviation of the mean by assuming that our sample is normally distributed. This would tell us, percentage wise, how close or how far the average US per capita consumption of egg is, in relation to the rest of the world.

To calculate the standard deviation, the negative deviations from the mean must be converted into positive values. When such a transformation is made, the

Table 3.7: Sample of Per Capita Egg Consumption by Country in 2000*

COUNTRY	Total (x)	Mean (x̄)	(x-x̄)	(x-x̄)²
Argentina	157	197.8545	-40.85454545	1669.094
Australia	155	197.8545	-42.85454545	1836.512
Austria	235	197.8545	37.14545455	1379.785
Belgium	204	197.8545	6.145454545	37.76661
Brazil	94	197.8545	-103.8545455	10785.77
Canada	184	197.8545	-13.85454545	191.9484
China (2)	232	197.8545	34.14545455	1165.912
Columbia	151	197.8545	-46.85454545	2195.348
Cyprus	218	197.8545	20.14545455	405.8393
Czech Re-pub.	296	197.8545	98.14545455	9632.53
Denmark	226	197.8545	28.14545455	792.1666
Finland (3)	153	197.8545	-44.85454545	2011.93
France	265	197.8545	67.14545455	4508.512
Germany	225	197.8545	27.14545455	736.8757
Greece	118.5	197.8545	-79.35454545	6297.144
Hungary	265	197.8545	67.14545455	4508.512
India	35	197.8545	-162.8545455	26521.6
Ireland	131	197.8545	-66.85454545	4469.53
Italy	224	197.8545	26.14545455	683.5848
Japan	320	197.8545	122.1454545	14919.51
Mexico	308	197.8545	110.1454545	12132.02
Netherlands	180	197.8545	-17.85454545	318.7848
Norway	173	197.8545	-24.85454545	617.7484
Portugal	182	197.8545	-15.85454545	251.3666
Russian Fed.	234	197.8545	36.14545455	1306.494
Slovakia	230	197.8545	32.14545455	1033.33
South Africa	111	197.8545	-86.85454545	7543.712
South Korea	191	197.8545	-6.854545455	46.98479
Spain	224	197.8545	26.14545455	683.5848
Sweden	193	197.8545	-4.854545455	23.56661
Switzerland	183	197.8545	-14.85454545	220.6575
U.K.	173	197.8545	-24.85454545	617.7484
USA	258.7	197.8545	60.84545455	3702.169
Total	6529.2		0.00	123248

*Data Source: The International Egg Commission, December 31, 2000. Total per capita consumption (i.e.) consumption per person includes shell eggs and equivalent egg products. Estimates for Austria, Cyprus, Italy, Japan, and South Africa are those of 1999.

absolute values are obtained. In absolute form, the sum of deviations is a counting number (i.e., not zero). When this total is divided by the number of entries or observations, the Mean Absolute Deviation (MAD, $\sum |(x-\mu)|/n$) is obtained.

Although MAD is informative and useful, the variance or standard deviation is normally preferred. The standard deviation is the square root of the variance and it closely approximates the MAD. The population variance is simply an average of squared deviations of scores from the arithmetic mean, normally denoted as sigma squared (σ^2) $= \sum (x-\mu)^2/n$ (the sum of squared deviations divided by the number of entries/observations). The variance of small samples underestimates the population variance and, therefore, to deal with that problem, the number of observations is reduced by one (n-1) as the denominator.

The notation for sample variance is normally given as $s^2 = \sum (x-\bar{x})^2/(n-1)$; notice that x bar ($\bar{x}$) replaces *mu* when discussing a sample variance. The standard deviation is just the square root of the variance. The notation for population variance is $\sigma^{1/2}$; and that for a sample, $s^{1/2}$.

The variance and standard deviation of per capita egg consumption in Table 3.7 could be calculated from column 5, which gives the squared deviations to cancel out the negative deviations from the mean. By itself, the variance (3851.50, $s^2 = \sum (x-\bar{x})^2/(n-1)$ does not render too much help in comparison to the standard deviation. By definition, the end result of the variance would always be colossal because all mean deviations are being squared to obtain positive numbers, but more so, bigger numbers get even bigger. To un-square the variance and make it more amenable to easy analysis, the standard deviation is preferred. It should be recalled that the standard deviation is the square root of the variance, which for our per capita egg consumption, is 62.06, a smaller number compared to the variance (3851.50).

One of the key advantages of the standard deviation is that it could be used to develop confidence intervals to assess the variation of data in relation to a perceived population (i.e.) to estimate the accuracy of the sample mean as a representation or microcosm of the population mean (this will be elaborated on in the next section). For example, a 90% confidence interval of an average is the range within which the population mean has a 90% chance of occurring. The smaller the standard deviation, the closer the observations are to the sample and expected population average.

Another important attribute of the standard deviation as a measure of dispersion is that if the mean and standard deviation of a normal distribution are known, the percentile rank of a given score could be computed on a standard scale using *z*-scores (discussed in the next section).

Using Chepachet's Theorem, $1 - [1/k^2]$, the proportion of data set lying within *k* standard deviations (*k*>1) of the mean, where *k* = the number of standard deviations, could be identified. For example, this theory suggests that 75% of a given or arbitrary data would be within 2 standard deviations of the mean.

The Standard Deviation and Central Limit Theorem

We have already learnt how to calculate mean, variance, and standard deviation of data. These measures could also be calculated with Excel by identifying the appropriate function and range of data entry (not values). For example, SUM (B3:B36) will give the total or sum of values in the cells B3 to B36; AVERAGE (B3:B36) will give the average of the values in those cells; VAR (B3:B36) will give the variance of values in those cells; and STDEV (B3:B36) will give the standard deviation of values in those cells. Note that these calculations should be made from the raw data itself without other forms of computations like MAD, or Error Sum of Squares (ESS).

The essence of this section is to discuss the standard deviation in the light of the Central Limit Theorem (CLT). The *CLT* describes the relationship between the sampling distribution of sample averages and the population that a sample is taken from. The main argument of the theorem is that if a sample size (n) is large enough, such that $n \geq 30$, then the sampling distribution of the sample averages should approximate the normal distribution. The larger the sample size the better the approximation should be. To facilitate a practical analysis, let us consider the prices of Statistical texts given in Table 3.8. How useful is the standard deviation?

Suppose we want to know how ***Robust Statistics*** (which costs $39.95) compares with the cost of other Statistics texts in the US. We would not be able to make such an analysis of the cost of ***Robust Statistics*** unless we have further information beyond its cost. Knowing that the average cost of Statistics texts in the US is $62.42 cents (i.e., the sum of all the prices of texts in the sample, $2122.39, divided by the number of texts or observations in the sample, 34) would help us to make a comparison of the cost of ***Robust Statistics*** with the average cost of statistics texts, and we could conclude that the cost of ***Robust Statistics*** is below the average cost of Statistics texts by about $22.47 cents (i.e., $39.95 - $62.42 = - $22.47). This difference does not say anything about the significance of the cost of the text in relation to all other statistics texts. This problem necessitates the reasoning that some form of distribution must be subsumed, and that we want to know how ***Robust Statistics*** stands in that distribution. We would therefore need to know the distribution of the standard deviation of the mean, assuming the distribution is normal or bell-shaped.

Fortunately, we know that 68% of the values of a normal distribution lie within 1 standard deviation of the mean because the majority of the values of a normal distribution are concentrated around the mean or average. Of the remaining 32%, an additional 27% accounts for 2 standard deviations of the mean (i.e., 68% + 27% = 95%), and an additional 4.7 % accounts for 3 standard deviations (i.e., 99.7%). Therefore, a value within 1 standard deviation would be closer to the mean, and values within 2 and 3 standard deviations would be farther away from the mean (see Figure 3.3).

Figure 3.3: The Standard Normal Distribution and Central Limit Theorem

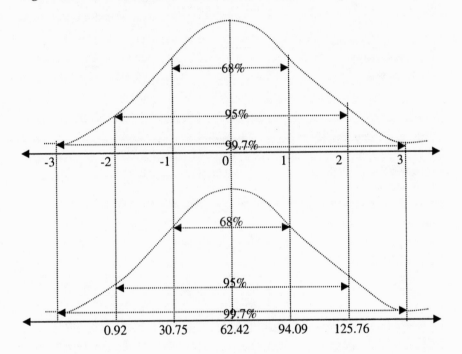

Table 3.8: Cost of Statistics Texts and Measure of Variation

Statistics Texts	Prices ($)	Mean $(\overline{X})$	$(x-\overline{X})$	$(x-\overline{X})^2$
Assessment Ability	79.95	62.42	17.53	307.19
Learning from Data	65	62.42	2.58	6.64
Regression Analysis	49.95	62.42	-12.47	155.58
Psychology of Consumer Behavior	30.95	62.42	-31.47	990.56
Structural Equation Modeling	40	62.42	-22.42	502.80
Statistics Unplugged	30.95	62.42	-31.47	990.56
Elements of Statistical Reasoning	73.95	62.42	11.53	132.87
Behavioral Statistics	102.95	62.42	40.53	1642.42
Cognitive Science	79.95	62.42	17.53	307.19
Guide to Behavioral Research	47.95	62.42	-14.47	209.47
Statistical Methods	49.95	62.42	-12.47	155.58
Statistics in Plain English	22.5	62.42	-39.92	1593.87
Bayesian Methods	69.95	62.42	7.536	56.65
A Student's Guide to ANOVA	26.95	62.42	-35.47	1258.35
Modeling Multilevel Data	75	62.42	12.58	158.18
Presenting your Findings	14.95	62.42	-47.47	2253.71
Reading Multivariate Statistics	29.95	62.42	-32.47	1054.51
Using Multivariate Statistics	140.6	62.42	78.18	6111.61
Discovering Statistics Using SPSS	38.95	62.42	-23.47	550.99
Essentials of Statistics	86.95	62.42	24.53	601.56
Statistics	105.95	62.42	43.53	1894.58
Statistics for Psychology	102.67	62.42	40.25	1619.80
Statistics For Dummies	14.77	62.42	-47.65	2270.83
Applied Longitudinal Data Analysis	69.5	62.42	7.08	50.08
Statistical Methods in Education	118	62.42	55.58	3088.78
Applied Multiple Regression	65	62.42	2.58	6.64
Analysis of Survey Data	95	62.42	32.58	1061.25
Statistical Applications	89.95	62.42	27.53	757.72
Student Friendly Statistics	34.4	62.42	-28.02	785.30
Statistics for Long-Memory	64.95	62.42	2.53	6.38
Research Methods	35	62.42	-27.42	752.03
Numerical Issues	89.95	62.42	27.53	757.72
Statistics in Psychiatry	39.95	62.42	-22.47	505.05
Robust Statistics	39.95	62.42	-22.47	505.05

The Standard deviation for the sample distribution is $31.67 (the square root of the variance, 1003.076). This is very useful information if we want to know whether the cost of **Robust Statistics** is considerably less than the average cost of all statistics texts in the US. If it is within 1 standard deviation, it is statistically close to the mean. The mean of the sample is $62.42. **Robust Statistics**, which costs $39.95, is, therefore, within 68% (1 standard deviation) of all values in the distribution. Prices ranging from $30.75 cents to $94.09 cents could be considered to be very close to the mean (1 standard deviation). This argument is depicted in Figure 5.3, which gives the standard normal bell-shaped curve and the distribution of Statistics texts based on the concept of normality.

The theory which enables us to compare our sample mean and sample standard deviation with the expected population mean and standard deviation is known as the Central Limit Theorem (CLT). The basic arguments of CLT could be summarized as follows: (i) For sample sizes (n) $\square$ 30 the sample distribution approximates the standard normal distribution (the greater the sample sizes the better the approximation); (ii) If the original data have a normal distribution, the sample mean ($\overline{X}$) will always have a normal distribution; and (iii) As the sample size (n) increases, the probability of making large errors decreases.

A research undertaking is normally incomplete or inadequate without a test of the findings. Today, there are all sorts of tests that could be done to evaluate coefficients (numerical values of characteristics or parameters after estimation); models (formal statements of theories which are usually in mathematical form); or hypotheses (unproven but testable statements or assertions).

A much more basic test that could be done is the hypothesis test which uses a standard score, alternatively known as z-score and associated with the normal distribution. There are of course other distributions like the t- distribution; F-distribution; and Chi-square distribution. For the purposes of this work, these distributions will not be given detailed attention here. It is however important to note that for small samples (i.e., less than 30 observations), the t-test, which is associated with the t-distribution, must be used.

With an underlying caveat of making two types of errors—Type I and Type II errors, the z-score enables the researcher to accept or reject a hypothesis. A Type I error refers to rejecting the null hypothesis when it is true, and a Type II error refers to failing to reject the null when it is false. Notice that we have said "failing to reject" and not "accepting" the null. By definition and convention hypotheses are not accepted. They are hypotheses and not tomb stone facts. There is a failure to reject because a procedure barely failed to reject the null.

The Standard Score (z-score) and Hypothesis Testing

Standard scores, which are also known as z-scores, are just another way of making individual-group comparisons. A standard score is just the number of standard deviation units an individual value or observation falls above or below the mean of a group or a collection of data.

The z-score is a rescaling mechanism of scores to make the mean of a z-score = 0, with a standard deviation of 1. A z-score is, therefore, consistent with the arguments of the standard normal distribution. The standard score also enables us to compare z-scores for different distributions. For example, we could compare the standard deviation of **Robust Statistics** in one distribution with its standard deviation in another distribution. The z-score is calculated by using equation 3.1.

$$z = (x-\bar{X})/s; \tag{3.1}$$

where x is an observed or hypothesized value; $\bar{X}$ is a sample mean; and s is a sample standard deviation. With enough information, the formula could be manipulated to solve for unknown values and make inferences by rewriting the formula. For example,

$$z(s) = (x-\bar{X}); \tag{3.2}$$

$$x = z(s) + \bar{X}; \tag{3.3}$$

$$\bar{X} = x - z(s); \text{ and} \tag{3.4}$$

$$s = (x-\bar{X})/z \tag{3.5}$$

The z-scores are needed to make inferences. Most, if not all good Statistics texts, have a table for the Standard Normal Distribution at the back of the text or on the inside of the front cover. Let us see if we can use the z-score to find out something about **Robust Statistics**. Suppose the mean of the costs of Statistics texts in the US is \$62.42 with a standard deviation of \$31.67, but the cost of **Robust Statistics** is \$39.95. What is the z-score? We could quickly solve this problem by using formula (3.1) above. Notice that the question requests a "z-score" and not the standard deviation (s) or a hypothesized value (x). It is important to know what question is to be answered and what formula should be chosen. Using formula 3.1 we can proceed as follows:

$$z = (39.95 - 62.42)/31.67 = -22.47/31.67 = -0.71. \tag{3.6}$$

The result (-0.71) confirms what we already know about the price of **Robust Statistics**. It is statistically close to the mean. The negative sign is a reminder that the cost is below the sample average. Yet, the price of **Robust Statistics** does not provide enough information about its significance in relation to the mean. To obtain further information a test would be warranted, and with that test, a hypothesis.

Knowledge of our z-score can be exploited to do a hypothesis test. The definition of the null hypothesis (Ho) is based on the premise of the research objective. For example, if the objective is a right tail test, (i.e., to test whether a measure is greater than a stipulated average), the null would usually be written as less than or equal to the value the researcher does not expect to find. The alternative is what the researcher expects to find. The primary objective would then be to reject the null (which is not always the outcome). The specification of a null hypothesis test would require an alternative (Ha) which would usually take one of three forms: (i) not equal to Ho; (ii) greater than Ho; and (iii) less than Ho.

The first specification of the alternate hypotheses would require a two-tail test. If the confidence level is set at 95% the rejection regions would add up to 5% (α); which for a two-tail test would be $\alpha/2$ or .025%. The critical z would be 1.96 for the 95% confidence region and 2.58 for the 99%. For a one-tail test—greater than Ho (right tail), or less than the Ho (left tail), the rejection region will be 5% and the critical z will be 1.645. This means that the area under the normal curve between 0 and 1.645 is 45%. The remaining 5% is the rejection region of the right half of the distribution. The entire area under the distribution must add up to one.

The power of the test measures the ability of the test to correctly reject the null hypothesis when the hypothesis is false (the probability of not committing a Type II error), where P (Type II error) = β. The power of the test is, therefore, 1-β usually 95% (i.e., the non rejection region).

The manager of a book store, say *Collegiate Enterprises*, might want to find out whether the price of **Robust Statistics** ($39.95), which is also the average price of 34 of his Statistics texts, is significantly less than the mean value of Statistics texts sold in the US ($62.42). The test could be formulated as follows:

$$\text{Ho:} \geq 62.42 \qquad \text{Ha} < 62.42$$

To do hypothesis testing with the z distribution, the z distribution should be used as a test statistic. This would require a slight modification of equation 5.1 so that the z distribution could be used as a test statistic (a value from sample information which is used to reject or not reject the null hypothesis). In test statistic form, the z distribution test statistic becomes:

$$z = (\bar{X} - \mu)/(\sigma/\sqrt{n}). \qquad (3.7)$$

Here $\bar{X}$ is the sample mean; μ is the population mean; σ is the standard deviation; and n is the sample size. Using equation 3.7 the test could be set up as:

$$z = (39.95-62.42)/(31.67/\sqrt{34}) = -4.14. \qquad (3.8)$$

The z-test statistic falls in the rejection area, and, therefore, the null is rejected. Apparently this test-statistic, which is not fundamentally different from the t-test statistic, shows that the difference is significant.

A similar analysis could be done for a right-tail test. Suppose a Statistics professor makes a claim that in order to pass Statistics, students must study Statistics more than 10 hrs a week (i.e., $H_0 \leq 10$; and the claim = $H_a > 10$). A student decides to evaluate the merit of the claim by sampling 34 Statistics students in Statistics College and discovered that on average successful Statistics students study 15 hrs a week with a standard deviation of 10. Is the professor's claim statistically viable at the 95% level of confidence ($\alpha = 0.05$)? (i) First find the test statistic:

$$z = (\bar{X} - \mu)/ (\sigma/\sqrt{n}) = (15-10)/(10/\sqrt{34}) = 2.94 \qquad (3.9)$$

(ii) Look up 2.94 in the Standard Normal Table: The p-value for 2.94 = 1-0.9981 = 0.002 (area to the right of z); and (iii) Compare p-values, 0.002 v. 0.05. With 0.002 < 0.05, the null is rejected. Alternatively, notice that 1.96 < 2.94, or 2.94>1.96 which puts the z-score in the rejection region; and (iv) Interpret the rejection decision. Based on the sample and a 95% level of confidence, there is enough statistical evidence to support the professor's claim that on average successful Statistics students study more than 10 hours a week. What type of error might have been committed?

The z-score could be used to do other important things: (i) To calculate the area under the standard normal curve (i.e., with mean = 0, and standard deviation = 1); (ii) To compare normal distributions; and (iii) To calculate margins of error when polling respondents. To undertake these tasks, it is important to know how to read the table of the standard normal distribution. A simple representation of the table normally takes the abbreviated form of Table 3.9:

Table 3.9: Abridged Standard Normal Distribution Table

z	.04	.05	.06	.07	.08	**.09**
0.0						**.5359**
0.1						
0.2						
0.3	.6331					

The standard normal distribution table should be read in terms of rows and columns. Table 3.9 has five rows (counting from top to bottom in a north-south direction) and seven columns (counting from left to right or vice-versa). The first row and first column provide z-scores after calculations using equation 3.1. The corresponding cells for each z-score give the value of z in percentage form. For example, let us assume that after calculating z, the answer is 0.09.

The corresponding value of the answer (0.09), in percentage form, is 54% (i.e., second row, seventh column 0.5359). This means that the area to the left of z is 54 percent (the shaded area of Figure 3.4). Notice that this makes sense because the mean is 0, and it divides the area above and below the mean of the normal curve into two equal halves; 0.09 is only about 4% beyond the midpoint. It is also worth remembering that the area under the normal curve equals 1 or 100%. If 54% has been accounted for, 46 % is unaccounted for. The area that is unaccounted for is the area to the right of z.

Figure 3.4: Area under the Normal Curve

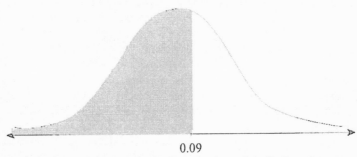

0.09

The procedure outlined above is equally instrumental to finding the area under the normal curve between two points. For example, suppose we want to find the area between 1.07 and -0.09. We would first need to get the two z values from the standard normal table. The value for z = 1.07 is .8577, and the value for z = -0.09 is 0.4641. Subtracting the smaller number from the bigger number will give us the area between the two z-scores (i.e., 0.8577- 0.4641 = 0.3936), which is 39% (see Figure 3.5)

Figure 3.5: Area under the Normal Curve

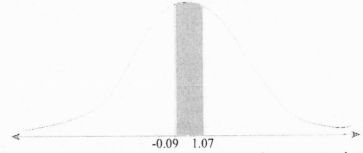

-0.09   1.07

In addition to finding the areas under the normal curve, the z-scores can be used to compare distributions. This is a very powerful tool at the disposal of the researcher.

Suppose a researcher is interested in the efficacy of Advil and Tylenol as painkillers in two US states, Texas and New York. He decides to do an intensive research as to which of the two drugs is superior for killing pain. After his re-search, he discovers that the average number of people for which Advil works better is 500. He interviews 1000 people in Texas and finds out that on average Advil works better for 600 people with a standard deviation of 50. He then sets up his z-score as follows: z = (600-500)/50 = 2.

Adopting the same procedure, the researcher conducts research for Tylenol and discovers that Tylenol works better, on average, for about 1500 people. From a New York sample of 3000 people, he finds that on average Tylenol works better for 2000 New Yorkers with a standard deviation of 350. He then sets up his findings as follows: z = (2000 − 1500)/350 = 1.43.

With the two z-scores, the researcher can then be able to tell which drug is a better painkiller using the standard normal curve. For Advil z = 2, which is 0.9772, and for Tylenol z = 1.43, which is 0.9236. The area to the left of z for Advil is greater (98%) than the area to the left of z for Tylenol (92%). In this case, he could then be able to conclude that Advil scores better as a painkiller by using the standard normal curve. This analysis could be extended if the re-searcher wants to test for the significance of the difference between averages by using a z-test statistic, which is the difference between the averages of the sam-ples divided by the square root of the combined ratio of the variances to the sample sizes.

The standard score could also be used for calculating the margin of error when conducting polls. Suppose a researcher is interested in a forthcoming Senatorial election and wants to know whether people will vote for the **Blue Party.** He luckily finds 1000 respondents to give him an honest answer to his question. His result indicates the following: 600 potential votes for the **Blue Party**. There is likelihood that his sample would have a margin of error even though he is assuming normality. To calculate the margin of error, he uses the following formula: $z* \sqrt{[p(1-p)/n]}$; where z is a z-score to capture the confidence level (1.96 = 95%), p is the sample proportion = 600/1000 = 0.6, and n= the sample size. The margin of error =0.030 = 3%. The z-score is, therefore, a very important facilitator of extensive research with a claim of normality. The next section deals with the estimation of data using regression analysis and making inferences.

Regression Analysis: Data estimation and Inference

A regression is a technique or method to estimate a model to determine relation-ships between variables and the viability of a theory and/or its component parts (variables) through inference (hypothesis test and conclusion). The estimation of a theory must, therefore, be guided by a model specification based on a theory. Apart from correlation, Granger-Causality, and Structural Vector Autoregres-sion (VAR) analyses, estimation would require some kind of structural specifi-cation consisting of a dependent variable and independent variable(s).

A dependent variable is usually found on the left-hand side (LHS) of an equation (except for the simultaneous system of equations when one or more could also be found on the right hand side, RHS). A dependent variable is the variable of interest to be explained and it is alternatively known as the regressand, response variable, endogenous variable, controlled/outcome variable or the predictand. It is the variable which depends on the behavior of other variables on the right hand side known as the independent, explanatory, predictor, control, or stimulus variables.

The structural form is then estimated by a regression method which is essentially the regression of the dependent variable on the independent variable(s). For example, a researcher might want to explain a theory of beer consumption, labor performance, population growth, and college enrolment. If the researcher is interested in explaining the behavior or performance of these variables, they become the dependent variables. Invariably, the question which follows is: On what factor(s) do these variables depend? The factor(s) which explain the behavior or performance of the variables of interest are the independent variable(s). Based on our prior choice of dependent variables, these could be price, taxes, and beer availability/supply (for consumption); education, age, wage rate; and gender (for labor); education, health care, food, and epidemic or wars (for population growth); and employment, tuition, scholarship, and wealth (for college enrolment). The researcher would then be obligated to find good and appropriate data on the variables (dependent and independent).

A typical representation of one of the models above would take the following regression specification:

$$\text{Beer Consumption (BC)} = a + \beta(\text{price}_{\text{beer}}) + \beta(\text{taxes}) + \beta(\text{supply}) + e \qquad (3.10)$$

Equation (3.10) shows that the researcher is interested in explaining beer consumption in terms of the price of beer, taxes on beer (a form of excise tax), and the amount of beer supplied. This is the intercept expression (i.e., the amount of beer that will be consumed when everything else is not given consideration, alternatively, when everything else is zero). The betas (β) are the coefficients of the variables to be estimated, otherwise, known as slope coefficients. They give numerical estimates of the estimated variables in terms of a rate of change (denoted as $\Delta y/\Delta x$, the rise over the run), which are then evaluated for their relevance or significance to the dependent variable using the t-test, the Wald coefficient test, or other appropriate tests. The e is for the amount of error, which is associated with the specification, implicitly assumed to be stochastic and normally distributed with a mean value of zero and constant variance. The typical regression model could, therefore, be broken up into two parts—the deterministic component, which excludes the error term (described in terms of the expected value of the dependent variable given the independent variable(s)); and the stochastic/random segment, which is captured by the error term.

The slope coefficients indicate by how much the dependent variable is changing when an independent variable changes by one unit. In Economics parlance or lingo, this is defined in terms of marginalism—the incremental (marginal) change of the independent variable on the dependent variable, a concept that is almost analogous to the concept of elasticity. Consider an extension of the thought. If the data are collected in percentage changes, the model is well specified with sufficient explanation of variation in the data, and the price coefficient of our beer consumption function is -0.05 and significant (t-stat $\square$ 2), a researcher can conclude that for a 1% increase in the price of beer, the consumption of beer is going to fall by 0.05 %. Such reasoning would affirm the expected inverse relationship. A variable which is significant should have a *t* value which is equal to or greater than 2. This also implies significance at the 95% level of confidence (very small margin of error $\square$5 %). These values are reported at the end of every regression under what is considered to be the analysis of variance (ANOVA).

Theory allows the researcher to anticipate whether the value/s of the coefficients in his regression should be positive or negative. For example, if normal behavior is assumed (i.e., assuming those beer consumers are not generally addicts), if the price of beer goes up, beer consumers should consume less beer due to income and substitution effects. As a result of the price increase, the purchasing power should fall and beer consumers should consume less, *ex post facto* (income effect). Some of the other related goods should now become comparatively cheaper or attractive, for example, *Guinness Stout*, wine, or *vodka* (substitution effect).

The price coefficient should, therefore, be negative and significant if the theory of inverse relationship is correct. This implies that as price goes up, beer consumption should fall. Taxes should have a similar effect but not the supply. When supply increases, (i.e., when supply changes to reflect an increase, or when the supply curve shifts to the right), the price falls and through the price mechanism, consumption should increase, other things being equal (*ceteris paribus*) suggesting a positive correlation. Regression analysis is more about correlation than causation. It would, therefore, be erroneous to imply that a price increase causes a reduction in beer consumption. Conventionally, it will be much more appropriate to associate the decline in beer consumption with a price increase.

In model specification, variables must be selected carefully to avoid biased estimation. In particular, there are at least two important pitfalls to be mindful of in the variable selection process of a simple linear regression model—*multicolinearity* and *heteroskedasticity*. *Multicolinearity* occurs when independent variables are correlated to such an extent that their impact on the dependent variable could not be successfully differentiated. For example, wealth and income are strongly correlated because wealth includes income. If the two are chosen to be independent variables, it will be difficult to separate their effects on a dependent variable.

Heteroskedasticity (different/*hetero* spread/*skedasticity*) occurs when the variance of the error (y-ŷ = e) is not the same for each of the independent variables (in which case, the error would not have a normal distribution); where y is a function of the independent variables, f (x), ŷ is the estimated or predicted value of y to be found on the regression line or population regression line (PRL), and e is the error term. If y = ŷ, then e must be zero (the required condition for *homoskedasticity*, same spread). The PRL is the expectation of the dependent variable population (sample or the entire population, assuming normality) based on the given or conditional variables, E (Y|X$_i$)). The functional representation is known as the conditional expectation function or the population regression function (PRF, E (Y|X$_i$ = f (X$_i$)= a +β...). *Heteroskedasticity* is usually affiliated with cross-sectional data, which deals with different observations and sizes at the same point in time.

Just as it is important to be mindful of the selection of independent variables, it is also important to watch for dependent variables, which lack variation in the data. To have a consistent slope for the linear regression model, it is highly suggested that a natural log estimation of the variables be used. In logarithmic form this would mean re-writing equation (3.10) as:

$$\ln (BC) = a + \ln \beta \ (price_{beer}) + \ln \beta log \ (taxes) + \ln \beta \ (supply) + e \qquad (3.11)$$

It is not unusual for the last expression, *e,* to be left out in model specification because it is obviously assumed to be zero and redundant.

It is probably apparent by now that the classical regression model makes specific assumptions. The following must be noted before a model is specified: (i) That the mean value of the error in a model specification is zero and has a normal distribution; (ii) There is no serial correlation, i.e., observations of the error term in one period do not show up in another time period or affect the error term in another period (the errors are uncorrelated with each other, for time series data); (iii) All explanatory variables are uncorrelated with the error term; (iv) The error term must have a constant variance, i.e., the variance of the distribution of the error term for each observation must be the same (homoskedastic); and (v) no explanatory variable should be a perfect linear function of another. Much more contemporaneous statistical packages have tests for the violation of these preconditions for good estimation.

Variables which have an exponent of one are considered nonlinear. When they are raised to an exponent greater than one they are considered quadratic. Regression models may be specified in various forms, and it may take slightly different connotations when the objectives and specifications are different. For example, although causal relationships are not typically implied in cross-sectional analysis, a forecasting model with two or more variables may be defined as a *causal forecasting model.*

The reason for the observance of the regularity conditions (assumptions) is simply to prevent biased estimation or spurious regression when ordinary least square (OLS), the popular method of estimating the regression coefficients (parameters), is used as a method of estimation. The goal is for OLS to be BLUE (Best linear unbiased estimator) by minimizing the sum of the squared vertical deviations of each point from the regression line. This regression line is, otherwise, known as the sample regression function (SRF) because a sample is what is realistically dealt with in running a regression. The true population is unobtainable, but it is hoped that this line could approximate the population; hence, the population regression function (PRF), which is the expectation of how the dependent variable is going to change on average given the expectation of the explanatory variable(s). The vertical distances between data points and the regression line are the errors, which must be minimized or made to be as small as possible (hence OLS). The data points are actual coordinates of the dependent and explanatory variable(s).

Bivariate regression models are two-variable models—one dependent and one independent); multivariate models have more than two variables and simultaneous models are models with a system of equations. When two variables are combined into one, an interactive variable is created. For example, if a researcher is interested in explaining national output (GDP), GDP could be a function of investment, education, consumption, government spending, and net exports (five independent variables). Alternatively, the researcher can combine education and investment to create an interactive variable, and, therefore, four independent variables.

Estimation of regression models might require the transformation of the raw data to meet the objective(s) of the researcher. Data could be compiled into averages of three or more years. It is important to note, however, that averages of shorter periods provide for persistence and make it feasible for one variable to be a better predictor of the other.

Simultaneous models are notorious for endogeneity problems when used for cross-sectional analysis, and serial correlation when used for time series analysis. Endogeneity problems arise when an independent variable in an equation of a system of equations is also a dependent variable in another equation of the system. Estimation of such models without rectification leads to biased results or spurious/nonsense regression. Luckily contemporary statistical software is designed to deal with such problems.

The classic procedure to deal with a simultaneity problem is the use of an instrumental variable—a variable that is correlated with the independent variables, but not the errors. A familiar estimator to deal with this type of problem is the 2-stage Least Squares (2sls), alternatively known as an instrumental variable (IV) estimator. Although lagged variables are easy instruments, they may not altogether be suitable. It is always a good idea to experiment with others which make theoretical sense.

The successful use of 2sls requires the observance of preconditions for identification. Identification is essential for numerical estimates to be obtained from structural models. As such, the model must not be overidentified or underidentified. It must meet the order and rank conditions: (i) The number of predetermined or independent variables excluded from an equation must not be less than the number of endogenous or dependent variables in that equation less one; and (ii) In a model with the same amount of dependent variables as there are equations, for example 3 and 3, an equation is identified if one nonzero determinant of the order (3-1)(3-1) can be constructed from the coefficients of the variables excluded from that particular equation, but included in the other equations of the model. The rank condition could be intimidating and makes for good academic exercise. Good estimating software, however, barely requires users to specify their instruments. Knowledge of the order and rank condition is, nevertheless, helpful to input information into the computer.

As part of the specification process, the researcher must then decide whether he wants to run his regression as a double log model (constant elasticity model), which gives a constant slope coefficient, a log-lin model, in which the slope coefficient measures the constant change in the dependent variable for a given change in the independent variable, or its lin-log counterpart.

Estimation without hypothesis testing is rarely complete. It is then incumbent on the researcher to test his coefficients or models appropriately. Most statistical packages are well suited to meet this challenge. For example, Eviews provides opportunities for a Wald Test, *heteroskedasticity* test, serial correlation test, Lagrange Multiplier test, Hausman test (for endogeneity), cointegration test, or even joint coefficient tests. The analysis of variance, which is immediately reported after a regression, also provides an indication of how well the model has performed. It is always a good idea to check whether the t-statistic is greater than 2 for significant coefficients at the 95% level of confidence.

It should be recalled that to do any hypothesis test, a null hypothesis is needed. The null is normally the equivalent of naught, meaning that the claim is not viable or true, and, therefore, is spurious or false. This is normally written as H_o (H-sub 0). The primary objective of the hypothesis test is to reject the null, so that claims could withstand the test of rejection.

Test selection largely depends on the suspicions or objectives of the researcher and not all tests are required. In contradistinction to the null, is the alternative/research hypothesis normally written as H_a. Whenever the null is rejected, the alternative holds. If, on the other hand, there is a failure to reject the null, the alternative hypothesis fails; which means that there is a failure to reject the null.

To fully exemplify the analysis of estimation and inference consider the following regression model. Suppose a researcher is interested in modeling poverty in the US as a function of education and income inequality from 1968-2003. The model could be specified as:

Log (Poverty) =log (education) + log (income Inequality/GINI) + e   (3.12)

There are, of course, specific benchmark measurements of poverty. An individual earning an income of less than a dollar a day can be considered to be poor. Poverty can also be computed as a weighted average of a level of income. In the US the Census Bureau estimated it at $4,190 in 1980, and $9,183 in 2002 for individuals who are under 65 years. Assume that the researcher is interested in the percentage of people below a 50 percent poverty level using his estimates and Census Bureau estimates of the poverty threshold.

Apart from other measures of income inequality, let us assume further that the Gini ratio, (A/(A+B)), is used to measure income inequality; where A is the percentage between perfect equality and complete inequality, and B the percentage of complete inequality. Educational attainment is measured by the percentage of people in the US over 25 years who have completed a Bachelor's Degree.

After running the regression, the researcher has a result which is reported in Table 3.10. The table provides an ANOVA and other important information about the regression procedure.

Table 3.10: Eviews Result of Regression 3.12

Dependent Variable: LOG (POV)				
Method: Least Squares				
Date: 08/28/05 Time: 19:15				
Sample: 1968 2003				
Included observations: 36				
Variable	**Coefficient**	Std. Error	**t-Statistic**	**Prob.**
LOG (EDU)	-1.675982	0.616918	**-2.716702**	**0.0104**
LOG (GINI)	5.394296	1.035659	**5.208565**	**0.0000**
C	12.52303	3.191860	3.923427	0.0004
R-squared	**0.634953**	Mean dependent var		1.511887
Adjusted R-squared	**0.612829**	S.D. dependent var		0.226002
S.E. of regression	0.140626	Akaike info criterion		-1.005776
Sum squared resid	0.652593	Schwarz criterion		-0.873816
Log likelihood	21.10397	**F-statistic**		**28.69970**
Durbin-Watson stat	0.542451	**Prob (F-statistic)**		**0.000000**

The table indicates the regression variables are estimated in log form: (log (pov), log (Edu), and log (Gini). It shows, at the very top, that the dependent variable is the log of poverty. It also shows that the estimating method is OLS. The number of observations is 36, which is enough to assume that the data has a normal distribution like that of Figure 3.3. It should be recalled that at least 30 observations are required to make a claim of normality. Since some of the details of the table are not immediately relevant to the purpose of this work, only the relevant ones will be discussed here.

The regression result shows that the two independent variables which have been selected are not only significant, but they arguably have the expected positive and negative coefficient signs. The coefficient for education is -1.67 with a *t*-statistic value of -2.71 (the ratio of the coefficient to the standard error), and a probability value of 0.0104. The education coefficient suggests that if there is a 1% increase in the number of people obtaining Bachelor's Degrees, poverty should fall by about 1.7%. The probability value (0.01) shows that the coefficient is highly significant at the 99% level of confidence.

The regression result also shows that income inequality is positively correlated to poverty and even stronger than education. If inequality increases by 1%, poverty increases by about 5%. Without education in the regression (not shown here), the increase would be about 2-3%. The coefficient is also highly significant with a t-statistic value of 5.21.

The R-squared is, otherwise, known as the goodness of fit of the fitted regression line to the data set. It is a coefficient of determination, which shows how well the sample regression line fits the data. It shows that 63% of the total variation in poverty is explained by the regression model. It is the ratio of the explained sum of squares (ESS) to the total sum of squares (TSS) where ESS is

$\Sigma \ (\hat{y}-\bar{y})^2$, the sum of squared deviation of the mean of y from its predicted value;

and TSS is $\Sigma \ (y-\bar{y})^2$, the sum of squared deviation of the mean value of y from the observed values of y.

The adjusted R-squared is an alternative coefficient of determination which takes into consideration the number of independent variables in the model and the degrees of freedom (the number of observations reduced by one). The lower the degrees of freedom, the less reliable the estimates are likely to be. In short, the adjusted R-squared, $\check{R}^2 = 1- \{((1-R^2)* \ (n-1))/(n-k-1)\}$, penalizes the researcher for adding unnecessary independent variables where n is the number of observations, and k is the number of coefficients to be estimated.

The *F*-test or Wald test could be used to ascertain or test whether all the coefficients in a regression are collectively zero. The null hypothesis that the coefficients (education and income inequality) are jointly zero is strongly rejected by the probability value of 0.0000. An *F*-statistic value of 3 or greater is usually sufficient to reject the null that the coefficients are jointly zero. In this regression, the *F*-statistic is 28.69970.

The Breusch-Godfrey Serial/Autocorrelation test is used to test the hypothesis that the error/residual terms are serially correlated (see Table 3.11). The alternative hypothesis would be the OLS assumption that the errors are not serially correlated. This test is much more appropriate for time series data when there is a presumption that successive observations are likely to exhibit intercorrelations over time, in which case the errors would not have a normal distribution. The null hypothesis of serial/autocorrelation is rejected with a probability value of 0.000020. This outcome is expected partly because the time interval between observations is greater than a day, week, or month, but also because annual percentage changes are used as a measure of the behavior of the variables.

Table 3.11: Breusch-Godfrey Serial/Autocorrelation Test

Breusch-Godfrey Serial Correlation LM Test:				
F-statistic	15.67941	Prob. F (2,31)		0.000020
Obs*R-squared	18.10358	Prob. Chi-Square (2)		0.000117
Test Equation:				
Dependent Variable: RESID				
Method: Least Squares				
Date: 08/31/05 Time: 06:41				
Presample missing value lagged residuals set to zero.				
Variable	Coefficient	Std. Error	t-Statistic	Prob.
LOG (EDU)	0.123093	0.450657	0.273141	0.7866
LOG (GINI)	-0.097715	0.755908	-0.129269	0.8980
C	-0.559207	2.331259	-0.239873	0.8120
RESID (-1)	0.859784	0.212025	4.055114	0.0003
RESID (-2)	-0.138579	0.212078	-0.653434	0.5183
R-squared	0.502877	Mean dependent var		1.92E-15
Adjusted R-squared	0.438732	S.D. dependent var		0.13659
S.E. of regression	0.102299	Akaike info criterion		1.59353
Sum squared resid	0.324419	Schwarz criterion		1.37360
Log likelihood	33.68449	F-statistic		7.83977
Durbin-Watson stat	1.595733	Prob (F-statistic)		0.00014

The Wald test that education is insignificant is rejected (see Table 3.12). The *F*-statistic value is 7.380469 and the probability value is 0.0104. In the Wald procedure, the unrestricted estimated coefficient is calculated to show the extent to which the unrestricted likelihood estimates fit the null hypothesis.

Table 3.12: Wald Test of Education Coefficient

Wald Test:			
Equation: Untitled			
Test Statistic	Value	df	Probability
F-statistic	7.380469	(1, 33)	0.0104
Chi-square	7.380469	1	0.0066
Null Hypothesis Summary:			
Normalized Restriction (= 0)	Value		Std. Err.
C (1)		-1.675982	0.616918

A much more simplified measure of the relationship between two variables that stands apart from regression is correlation analysis, which is usually a measure of strength and direction.

Correlation Analysis

A correlation indicates the relationship between variables. This relationship is normally analyzed in terms of two variables in an x-y-space: the dependent or response variable (y), and the independent or explanatory variable (x). A caveat is immediately warranted because of the use of the words "dependent" and "independent." Correlation does not show dependence of one variable on the other as one might expect in ordinary regression analysis. It does not imply causation either. It barely shows relationships. Apart from not having any relationship between variables, one would expect to find the following relationships: (i) Negative linear relationship; (ii) Positive linear relationship; and (iii) Nonlinear or quadratic relationship. Using a scatter plot, these relationships are shown in Figure 3.6.

A negative correlation shows that as the values of y increase, the values of x decrease for ordered pairs of y and x. The opposite of a negative correlation is a positive correlation, which shows that after the values of x, and y is plotted in order as the values of y increase the values of x also increase. A nonlinear correlation shows a continuous positive and negative relationship (parabola), or a continuous negative and positive relationship. When data points are scattered all over the x and y spaces, a correlation cannot be established and the relationship is independent.

Figure 3.6: Correlation of Variables

<u>Negative Correlation</u>   <u>Positive Correlation</u>   <u>Nonlinear Correlation</u>

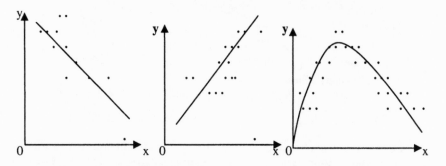

  To measure the type and strength of the direction of the linear relationship between two variables, the correlation coefficient (r) is used. This is normally the sample correlation coefficient denoted by the formula:

$$r = [\, n\sum xy - (\sum x)(\sum y)\,] / [\sqrt{n}\sum x^2 - (\sum x^2)] * [\sqrt{n}\sum y^2 - (\sum y)^2] \qquad (3.13)$$

where r is the Pearson product moment correlation coefficient (a test statistic); n is the number of pairs of data; y is the dependent variable; and x is the independent variable.

  The range of the r is between -1 and 1. A positively strong relationship will be close to one and a negatively strong relationship will be close to -1. A correlation coefficient which is close to zero shows a weak correlation or none at all.

  The t-test can be used to conduct a hypothesis test of strength or significance. The standardized test statistic is:

$$t = r/[\sqrt{(1-r^2)/(n-2)}]. \qquad (3.14)$$

The population correlation is given as rho (ρ) and the tests could be stipulated as follows:

   (i) $H_0: \rho \geq 0$ (ii) $H_0: \rho \leq 0$ (iii) $H_0: \rho = 0$
     $H_a: \rho < 0$ $H_a: \rho > 0$ $H_a: \rho \neq 0.$

The procedures for the hypothesis tests are consistent with our earlier discussions.

  The essence of this chapter has been to provide basic information about the research process, data analysis, estimation, and inference. The next chapter addresses, plagiarism, the basic writing process, and tips for writing research papers.

PART III: COMMON ASSIGNMENTS IN CLASSES

CHAPTER 4

PLAGIARISM AND RESEARCH PAPERS

What is Plagiarism?

Plagiarism is stealing someone else's work and passing it off as one's own. Plagiarism is the direct use of four or more exact words in a row. However, some professors will argue that plagiarism is the use of three or more words from a text without a reference to the author or source. Copying and pasting a text from a website is another form of plagiarism. For this reason, it is important to be extra careful when copying or when using sources.

Ways People Plagiarize

Students try many tricks to plagiarize. As stated earlier, it is not worth it to try to plagiarize. Below are some ways students try to plagiarize:

Case 1. If a student has trouble with English, especially English as a Second Language (ESL), he or she sometimes copies full paragraphs or sentences that are in perfect English. The problem is that the rest of the text has many grammatical and/or ESL errors throughout it. The plagiarized sections stand out clearly as not the student's own work.

Case 2. Some students, especially freshman and sophomores, prefer to use websites that will write their papers for them. These websites will guarantee that the paper being requested will be written exactly as specified. Another version of case 2 is to use someone else's paper and pass it off as one's own. However, professors know that students do not write these papers on their own because most students do not have the vocabulary and knowledge to write in such a sophisticated way. Also, instructors can tell when a paper is plagiarized by comparing the writing in a student's paper to the writing in in-class assignments.

Case 3. Some students do not cite references. They use quotations, but do not reference from the source of the quotation. In other instances, students use information from journals without citing them. Consider two examples:

According to Smith, "The debate on evolution has created a dichotomy among religious people and scientists."

The previous sentence is an example of **plagiarism** because it has no citation. The following example is the opposite of a plagiarized sentence:

According to Smith, "The debate on evolution has created a dichotomy among religious people and scientists" (Smith, 1998, p. 24).

The Consequences of Plagiarism

There are severe consequences for plagiarism. Everyone has read about professors and authors who have lost credibility because of this issue. Just as professionals can get in trouble, so can students. At best, students who plagiarize will receive an "F" for that course. If the student is lucky, the instructor might let the student redo the assignment. In the worst-case scenario, if the professor wants to take further action, he or she can have the student expelled from school. Regardless, the student's records are permanently marked. This hurts anyone who decides to pursue a masters and a doctorate.

What Needs to Be Cited?

The most popular question regarding plagiarism is: What needs to be cited? Anything that is not common knowledge needs to be cited. This includes statistics, direct quotes, graphs, and information that a large majority of people does not know. It is better to overcite than to not cite enough. Therefore, if you are unsure of whether to cite, it is better to put a citation where you found the information.

Ways to Prevent Plagiarism

With a little effort, plagiarism can be prevented. One way is to develop summarizing skills. Another is paraphrasing. Paraphrasing is best way to put a text into one's own words. This will be discussed later.

The other way is to punctuate quotations in the appropriate way. A big mistake students make is that they use too many quotations. Too many quotations mean that there is very little of the students' own words. In reality, he or she has not really written much. Below are examples of how to use quotations.

The Double Quotation Mark

Use the double quotation mark ("...") when including direct quotes.

John said, "He was not able to perform his best today." "John was not able to perform his best today," he said.

"John was not able," he said, "to perform his best today."
Indirect quotations never require quotation marks.

John stated that he was not able to perform his best today.
An exception to the double quotation mark is a long quote. A long quote is a quote of four lines or more. Do not use quotation marks when using long quotes. How one includes a long quote in a paper depends on what citation style his or her professor has asked instructed to use and the conventions of the particular academic field. When a quote is four lines or more, and the APA style is required, use the colon and indent it 10 spaces (2 tabs) from both margins.

The following passage illustrates this theory (Smith, 2003):

-------------. (p. 34)

When a quote is four lines or more in MLA style, use the colon and indent it 10 spaces (2 tabs).

The following passage illustrates this theory (Smith):

---------------. (34)

The Single Quotation Mark

When including a quotation that was itself quoted in the source, use single quotations to indicate this is not the work of the writer being quoted.

John said, "money is objectionable since 'money is the root of all evil' in contemporary human relations."

Square Brackets

Square brackets (**[...]**) are used to make changes to a direct quotation when necessary to maintain clarity.

John said, "We need some [more] people to speak up about the problems in the factories."

Ellipses

Ellipsis dots (...) are used when one wants to omit parts of a direct quotation. Wherever the ellipsis dots are, the second part must not break the flow of the sentence from the first part. There are **only** 3 dots used in ellipsis dots.

The general said, "He is a good man...but his military record has some questions that need to be answered."

Parentheses

Parentheses (**(...)**) are used to define abbreviation, indicate a page number, and paraphrase information.

The American Psychological Association (APA) is the preferred format for citing references in the sciences.

The following example illustrates the use of a parenthesis to indicate a page number after a short quote in APA format.

Steve states, "There needs to be more work done on this type of research" (p. 6).

Alternatively, an MLA format will take the following form:

Steve states that, "There needs to be more work done on this type of research." (6)

In-text citations also require the use of parentheses for paraphrasing information. Each style (MLA, APA, Chicago Style Manual) has a different method of citing references.

APA: Jones argues that the best approach to teaching punctuation is to know sentence patterns (Smith, 1999).

MLA: Jones argues that the best approach to teaching punctuation is to know sentence patterns (Smith, 19).

BASIC WRITING PROCESS

Writing is a process that is completed in steps or phases. However, they do not necessarily have to occur in a fixed order. The three phases are to be completed in the following order: (a) pre-writing; (b) writing; and (c) editing or revising.

Pre-Writing

Pre-writing, the process of generating ideas before the actual writing begins, involves two steps: (a) brainstorming and (b) planning or outlining. In pre-writing, the only things that are to be done are THINKING and PLANNING. *Brainstorming* is the first step in pre-writing. During brainstorming, the writer comes up with ideas to expand on. The process of generating ideas can be done in several ways:

      a.   putting oneself in the particular situation;
      b.   start with an example or illustration; and
      c.   reading academic texts.

For example, putting oneself in the situation requires that one generate questions that can be asked in context. A question that can be asked in context is: *What would I do if were in the therapist or social worker in this context?* Starting with an example or illustration can be a case study in social work or an example from a scientific study in a psychology journal. Reading academic texts is probably the best way to get ideas for papers. This is because academic texts contain recent research and topics in a particular field of study.

Now, one has to take these ideas that were brainstormed, and categorize them into reasons and supporting details. Here is the process with the same example. The writer has to ask him or herself several questions:

      a.   What is a reason and what is a supporting detail?;
      b.   What reason(s) best support(s) my thesis?; and
      c.   What is/are the most important reason(s)?

To show the process of how to write a research paper and the finished product, it is better to focus on one topic. Therefore, for the remainder of this chapter, the essay that will be the focus is "Stereotypes of Mexican Americans and how it affects their educational attainment". A list of ideas for this essay would look like Figure 4.1.

Figure 4.1: Organizing Ideas for Writing

Bilingual education
Ten most popular history textbooks
Immigration
Pre-Columbian
Media
Texas
WW I, WWII, and Korean War
Segregation
Minorities in textbooks

The second part of pre-writing is *planning* or *outlining*. This is where one takes the ideas from brainstorming and organizes them into an outline. Then, he or she sees if they can be developed into detailed paragraphs to support the thesis statement. One way to do this is using the informal outline in Figure 4.2. A formal outline (Figure 4.3) will be more specific with extra details. Even though the writer has come up with several possible supporting reasons, it does not mean that he or she can fully develop them. Many students skip this part of the process; as a result, their supporting reasons are usually not developed enough.

Here are some questions that a writer must keep in mind when planning:
- a.   Who is the intended audience?; and
- b.   How do these supporting ideas relate to the thesis statement?

Without these questions, many students stray from the thesis statement. That is why planning and outlining is extremely important.

When writing, the student should put him- or herself as the reader. The reverse is also true: When reading, the student should put him- or herself as the writer. This way, he or she will know what the contents of the will be essay before writing it to ensure that the body paragraphs and supporting reasons can be fully developed.

Figure 4.2: An Informal Outline

I.		Ten most popular history textbooks
	A.	Pre-Columbian
	B.	Texas
	C.	WW I, WWII, and Korean War
	D.	Segregation
	E.	Minorities in textbooks
II.		Media
III.		Immigration
IV.		Bilingual education

Figure 4.4 shows an example of an outline for a body paragraph. Each one of the sentences in this outline can be explained by the wh-questions (who, what, where, when, why, and how). The topic sentence answers the question *what*. The supporting details primarily answer the questions *why* and *how*. They can also answer the questions *who*, *when*, and *where*. The wh-questions are very important in developing supporting reasons. By asking oneself these questions, he or she can develop supporting reasons much easier because these questions will be answered.

One can ask several questions that can link and organize sentences together: (a) What is the purpose of adopting this idea?; (b) What solutions do you propose to the problem at hand?; and   (c) How does this problem affect the audience?

Figure 4.3: A Formal Outline

Thesis: What teachers read affects how they view their Mexican-American students.

I.   Print Media
       A.   History textbooks
              1.   Textbook influences
                     a.   Textbook sales
              2.   Mexico and Pre-Columbian era
                     a.   Not mentioned in textbooks
              3.   Mexicans in wars
                     a.   One-sided view point
                     b.   Braceros
              4.   Minorities
                     a.   Little detail given to accomplishments of minorities
       B.   Segregation in schools
              1.   Méndez trial
              2.   Propositions 187, 209, 227
II.   News Media
       A.   Negative images
              1.   Immigration
              2.   Movies
III.   Bilingual Education
       A.   Negative aspects of bilingual programs

Figure 4.4: An Outline of a Body Paragraph

Sentence 1: Topic sentence (TS) (What?)

Sentence 2: Explain TS (How? and Why?)

Sentence 3: Explain sentence 2 (How? and Why?)

Sentence 4: Explain sentence 3 (How? and Why?)

Sentence 5: Illustration and/or more support *(optional)*

Sentence 6: Explains how illustration is related to TS *(optional)*

Sentence 7: Sentence to conclude paragraph and/or introduces next paragraph

(Source: A. Martínez, J. C. S. C.)

Writing

The second part of the writing process is *writing*. WRITING is the only activity that is done in this phase. There are three parts to any text: (a) introduction, (b) body, and (c) conclusion.

The **introduction** is the part of any text that sets up or prepares the reader for what the text will be about. It is the first part of a paper, which includes: (a) background information; (b) the thesis statement or a restatement of thesis statement; and (c) any general statements to orient the reader to the topic, which are optional. It should be noted that the thesis statement focuses on only one major idea. The thesis statement does not always have to be in the introduction. Instead of being the introduction, it can be in the conclusion as it is in most academic texts. Another possibility is that it can be stated in both the introduction and the conclusion.

Some students have problems starting papers. If this is the case, it may be better for them to start with the body and write the introduction last. This way, the writer can start the paper without losing any time.

Body paragraphs contain all the details, support, arguments, and explanations about the thesis statement. The first sentence is usually the *topic sentence*, a general sentence that explains what the paragraph will discuss; it contains no details. The topic sentence does not have to be the first sentence of a body paragraph. The rest of the paragraph contains the details and explanations that support the topic sentence. The writer just has to put his or her fragmented ideas into complete sentences.

Explaining each preceding sentence develops a body paragraph. Each sentence needs to be explained by asking oneself one of the following questions:

    a.   What does this mean?;
    b.   Why is this important?; and
    c.   How?

Each body paragraph contains only one idea, and it must contain at least four sentences. However, there is no maximum limit on the number of sentences in a body paragraph. The first body paragraph does not restate the thesis statement because it follows the introduction. However, the body paragraphs following the first body paragraph need to have the thesis statement restated somewhere in the topic sentence because they are too far from the introduction. Within each paragraph, the sentences must be linked by transitions, as well as between each paragraph.

A body paragraph (Figure 4.3) is similar to the format of an essay. The topic sentence is the introduction. The body is the supporting reasons. The conclusion is the transition to the next sentence or the concluding sentence(s).

The **conclusion** is the final part of a paper. It briefly states the thesis statement and the supporting reasons. It may also contain any suggestions for future research or any opinions depending on the purpose of the paper.

It should be noted that the number of sentences of a paragraph or the length of the paper is in terms of its function. If there are different sections to it, subheadings need to be added. This will orient the reader. Also, what is described above is the basic format for any paper. What the reader has to do is format his or her paper to the necessary style and format of its function.

Editing

Editing and revising are probably the most difficult tasks in writing. This is because the writer may have difficulty subjectively and objectively reading his or her work. He or she knows exactly what is being discussed; familiarity with the his or her work may lead the student to not see omissions or errors that would stand out to a new reader. For this reason, the writer needs to have a trusted set of people that can read his or her works.

Below are the criteria for how all papers are frequently graded. The only differences between this set of criteria and others are that this is a general set of criteria and the others are based on a specific essay or assignment. They are in their order of importance:

1. **Focus**. Make sure the paper is focused around one major idea (thesis statement).
2. **Organization.** The paper needs to follow a logical order or sequence.
3. **Development**. Check to see that each paragraph supports only one idea and is fully developed.
4. **Language use**. Make sure that the vocabulary you use is appropriate. Make sure that no word is repeated too many times unless it is a technical word.
5. **Punctuation and spelling**. Make sure all sentences end with the appropriate end punctuation mark. Also, make sure all punctuation is correct. Check for spelling errors as well.
6. **Grammar**. Make sure that everything is grammatically correct. Also, make sure that every sentence has a subject and a verb, and that there are no sentence fragments (dependent clauses).

One way to edit is to read the essay to oneself. When the writer hears what he or she has written, it is easier to detect anything that sounds awkward. The student should make sure that he or she has read what is actually written and NOT what was intended to or thought to be written.

When reading over an essay for revision, the student should keep these criteria in mind. Figure 6 is an evaluation sheet with the major points to look for. The Peer Editing Evaluation Sheet is divided into two parts: the essay level and the paragraph level. At the essay level, the thesis statement is the most important thing. If there is no thesis statement, then there is no focus to the essay. The second most important thing to look at when editing is the organization of the essay. An essay still has to look aesthetically pleasing to the reader. Organizing all the paragraphs, figures, pictures, and tables in a way that is easy to follow does this. The third most important thing when revising an essay is the content.

At the paragraph level of the essay, paragraph development takes precedent. As stated earlier, each body paragraph needs to have a topic sentence and contain, at least, four sentences. Then, language use (appropriate vocabulary) comes into play. The very last thing that is looked at is the grammar, spelling, and punctuation. If the grammar, spelling, and punctuation are very distracting, they will come before anything else when editing.

Tips for Revising and Editing

The following are tips for paragraph development and Organization:
1. Make sure that the paper has a clear focus, thesis statement.
2. Make sure that each paragraph has only one idea. If there is more than one idea in a paragraph, put those ideas into separate paragraphs.
3. Make sure that each paragraph follows a logical and sequential order.
4. Make sure that all body paragraphs have, at least, four sentences. There is no maximum number. It is important not to focus on counting how many sentences. Only include enough information to get the point across.

Salient grammar and punctuation tips are:
1. Does every sentence have a subject and a verb? If any sentences start with a words such as *because* or *if*, and it is the only clause, then they are fragments because there is only a dependent clause. Make sure that all sentences have, at least, one independent clause.
2. Make sure that the essay does not shift tenses. In other words, make sure that if the verbs are in present tense, past tense is not used. The only time a writer can use another tense is if he or she transitions in and out of an example, research, or a situation.
3. Make sure that all verbs are in the correct form. For example, all regular past participles must end in *–ed*.
4. Make sure that all sentences end in end punctuation marks. Also, make sure that when combining sentences, they have the proper punctuation such as commas and semicolons.

Hierarchy of Grammatical Errors

When instructors look at students' essays for grammatical errors, they need to go through a hierarchy of grammatical errors (Figure 5). The hierarchy starts with the most basic grammatical errors such as subject and verbs, and progresses to the most advanced grammatical errors such as subjunctive mood. The teacher should address them in the order of importance based on frequency and how basic the grammatical error is. The more basic the error (tier 1 in Figure 4.5), the more egregious the error is. When professors see this type of error, they send their students to the writing or tutoring center to get help. They will also lower the grade on essays that contain these errors.

Figure 4.5: Hierarchy of Grammar and Punctuation Errors

Grammatical and Punctuation errors	Examples when looking at essays
Tier I: Basic Sentence Structure Errors, and Subjects and Verbs	Every sentence has a subject and a verb Using the appropriate pronoun Singular and plural nouns Subject-verb agreement Intersentential punctuation Upper- and lower-case letters Correct verb tense Tense shifting Intrasentential punctuation
Tier II: Pronoun Agreement	Pronoun agrees with its referent or antecedent
Tier III: Articles	Using the correct articles
Tier IV: Prepositions	Using the correct prepositions

Students should always keep several things in mind when they write their papers. What they should do is always keep a checklist in their minds as they write. In other words, they should put themselves as a reader when they write, and they should also put themselves as a writer when they edit their papers. The editing evaluation page (Figure 4.6) guides the writer to how the reader will look at his or her paper.

Figure 4.6: Editing Evaluation Sheet

Name	
Essay Level	**Comments**
Thesis	
Organization	
Content	
Paragraph Level	**Comments**
Development	
Language Use (appropriate word choice)	
Grammar, Spelling, and Punctuation	

Tips for Writing Research Papers

1. Start your research paper as soon as you get the assignment. The earlier you start it, the more time you have to work on it.
2. When starting a key word search, find an article or book that is close to the desired topic of interest. Use those key words in the abstract to help narrow your search. Once the key article/book is found, use those references at the end of it to find others.

3. Always have more references than necessary. It is always easier to take references away than it is to add them to research papers.
4. Organize your research according to your outline.
5. Research papers should be double-spaced unless specified by your instructor.
6. All papers should be revised several times. Utilize the university's tutoring/writing center. Most university tutoring centers are free, meaning that this service is included in the tuition.
7. Make sure you have followed the format your professor requested: writing style (APA, MLA, etc.), number of pages, years of reference, and number of references (see samples at the end of the chapter. Note that bold lettered words are for emphasis of key ideas and not part of the styles).
8. Ensure that your research is citing recent works. In general, research more than five years old is considered too old; however, some disciplines want it even more recent, not older than two years. Although recent references are preferred, there are times that one may have to revert to older references. Some cases include: historical studies and research topics that have not been researched for a period of time.
9. Learn to summarize academic essays and journal articles and be critical to zero in on key concepts and avoid redundancies or plagiarism.

Summaries and Critiques

Summarizing is one of, if not, the most difficult assignment in college. A *summary* is a brief synopsis of a text. The student must completely understand the text in order to write a summary. The format of the texts has been discussed in Chapter 2. In addition to understanding the text, the student has to be careful not to plagiarize (see Chapter 5); there are no exceptions. In other words, summaries have to be in one's own words. Summaries go by different names: summary, executive summary, abstract, discussion, conclusion, and literature review. Also, when a professor instructs his or her students to write a one-page abstract for a certain article, it really means that he or she wants a one-page summary of an article.

As a student is reading a textbook or essay, all he or she has to do is write one to two sentences beside the each important paragraph. This is called *annotating*. Annotations are not only good for summaries, but they also are notes that let the student know where a certain topic is discussed in the text. By putting these annotations together in the order they are written in the margins, the student is creating a summary of the text. This will save one a lot of time when it comes to understanding a text for a test or an assignment.

How to Summarize General Academic Essays

A summary of a general academic text must include the thesis statement and supporting ideas and major details. Summaries are always in present tense. One never puts his or her opinion in a summary. Opinions are critiques which are discussed later in this chapter. Parts of a summary can be in past tense when the methods and results of a scientific study are being discussed. No examples or minor details are included either.

SAMPLE SUMMARY OF A BOOK

Rodriguez in "Aria" explains the difference of having a public and private self. The difference is that having a public self involved speaking English where he was shy. He does not feel that he belongs in the school and on the streets in his neighborhood. The terror of just hearing people speak English makes him stay at home all the time. Having a private self is different for Rodriguez. He emphasizes that he can only have a private self at home. This is where he feels welcomed, close to his family.

Rodriguez feels that speaking English is very powerful because it shows that the person can communicate with the "gringos". Rodriguez says, "It was unsettling to hear my parents struggle with English. Hearing them, I'd grow nervous, my clutching trust in their protection and power weakened" (p. 15). In this quote, he is talking about how self-conscious he is that his parents do not speak English very well, but they try. At the same time, he feels that since his parents can hardly speak English, he is not well protected from the "gringos" and is weak. Rodriguez thinks of himself as being weak because, in this country, if one does not speak English well enough, he or she cannot get what he or she needs such as going to any government offices, hospitals, or even the grocery store.

How to Summarize Journal Articles

The basic principle for summarizing a general academic text is the same for a journal article. However, due to the nature of the material in a journal article, there are differences. The easiest way to summarize a journal article is to follow the format of the discussion. The *discussion* is what the whole journal article is about. For the participants and procedures, the student will have to go back to the methods section of the article.

If we notice each section of the article used with each summary, it is in accordance to the American Psychological Association (APA) in-text citations. It is important to state the author and the year of the article in focus, or it is considered plagiarism. This is how a student should approach his or her summary. *Present tense* is used for the purpose and problem statement, and the conclusion of the study. *Past tense* is used for explaining what the procedures and results of the study. It is easier to use the information (findings and implications) in the discussion as an outline for your summary.

Words to Use When Summarizing a Text

maintains	argues	states	purports
explains	concludes	shows	proposes
according to	illustrates	concerns	contends
expresses			

Sample Ways to Summarize a Journal Article

Introduction. The Cycles approach focuses on suppressing error patterns via targeting child's awareness and the use of the meta-linguistic attributes such as auditory bombardment and sound perception (Hodson, 2000).

    Methods. In Dodd & Bradford (2000), they used blablablablabla and la where they were able to distinguish between delayed developmental (DD) children and children with non-development (ND) error patterns. The children who made errors characteristic of younger normal-developing children were considered DD and those who made non-developmental error patters were ND.

    Discussion. Powell et al. (1991) suggest that stimulability is a strong predictor of a child's ability to …

Writing Your Own Abstract from Several Abstracts

This assignment involves extracting each purpose and problem statement from each abstract of a journal article, and come up with one purpose and problem statement from them.

Sample Abstract for a Proposal

The ultimate goal of phonological intervention is to suppress phonological processes and to be intelligible in connected speech. Stimulability is suggested to be a strong predictor of a child's ability and readiness to learn new sounds that are absent from his/her phonetic inventory. In addition to selecting sound targets, clinicians are faced with selecting different treatment approaches. In this study, four Mexican boys, aged 4.0-4.5, will undergo treatment. Each will receive a separate treatment: ART, MET, a combination of ART and MET, and no treatment. The results will be compared and the question of which is the best treatment will be answered. The expected outcome is that ...

Literature Reviews

Literature reviews are a brief synopsis of what research is in a particular field of study. This is the introduction to proposals and journal articles. Literature reviews go by different names: executive summaries, background information, introduction, and literature reviews.

Sample Literature Review for a Proposal

Unintelligible speech in childhood is often characterized by the use of unusual or deviant (i.e., non-developmental) phonological processes such as initial consonant deletion. These processes are reported to appear at speech onset and undergo little spontaneous change during the preschool years. The ultimate goal of phonological intervention is to produce intelligible speech during spontaneous discourse. In order to achieve this goal, clinicians have been generally advised to target phonemes that are stimulable. According to Powell et al. (1991), stimulability is suggested to be a strong predictor of the child's ability and readiness to learn new sounds that is absent from his/her phonetic inventory. Likewise, the study also found that phoneme- specific stimulability elicited "generalization" patterns whereby improvement was observed in all stimulable sounds regardless of treatment target. However, this a controversial issue because some authors give priority to non-stimulable sounds during treatment planning, or select processes that affect earlier-developing sounds as initial targets, while others select stimulable and non-stimulable sounds as targets (Miccio, Elbert, & Forrest, 1999; Powell et al., 1991). Therefore, it is important to evaluate, assess and test for stimulability in order to know what phonemes will best benefit from intervention.

In addition to selecting sound targets, clinicians are faced with selecting different treatment approaches. Treatments for phonological processes vary in areas of focus. Some are based on the principle of suppressing error processes (CYCLES approach), while others on motor programming skills. Since there is a gap in research as to which treatment is best for bilingual children with phonological disorders (PD), it makes it difficult for bilingual speech-language pathologists (SLPs) to effectively choose a method that will suit their clients' needs. In this study, three different phonological treatment programs will be administered to three bilingual children who possess developmental speech disorders and the outcomes will be compared, while one child will receive no treatment. It is hypothesized that a bilingual child who undergoes therapy combining two treatment approaches will best be effective from the other children who are only exposed to one therapeutic intervention. The results will demonstrate that a combination of both treatments will increase the subject's intelligibility.

Critiquing

A critique is also called a *reaction* or an *opinion*. Many college students confuse this assignment to be a summary. This is to be written in past tense. When critiquing a general **academic text**, the first thing to do is to look at the thesis statement. Everything else such as the supporting reasons and details must be in conjunction to the thesis statement. When the thesis statement, supporting reasons and details are located, the student needs to evaluate how well the supporting reasons and details support the thesis statement. A good article to read about critiquing journal articles is:

Kuyper, B. (1991). Bring up scientists in the art of critiquing research. *BioScience, 41*(4), 248-250.

When critiquing a **journal article**, the basic principle is the same as a general academic text. Each section is looked at separately.

The reader needs to find the purpose and problem statement (what the study is about) to define his **introduction**. Once the statement of purpose is found, the next thing to look at is the previous studies. Previous studies show what research has been done. The previous studies must build up to why the article was written.

The **methods** section needs to explain how the participants were chosen. It also needs to describe the different test and stimuli that was used in the article. The reader has to determine if the subjects were the right ones for the study, if the tests and stimuli were appropriate for what the researchers' purpose and problem statement.

The **results** need to be summarized in order of importance. The most important results have to come first.

The **discussion** should summarize the other sections and make recommendations for future research.

Sample APA Paper

History and the Portrayal 1

Title   History and the Portrayal of Mexican-Americans

Student's Name   Steven Jones

Course Number   ESC 769

Professor's Name   Professor Martinez

Due Date   May 15, 2001

History textbooks, books, journals, personal experiences, and magazines are the primary ways that children learn about their history and other groups' histories (Salvucci, 1991 & Rodriguez, 1999). If one reads American history books and other books on Mexico, Mexicans, and Mexican-Americans, that person would possibly leave with a negative image of Mexico, Mexicans, and Mexican-Americans **(Salvucci, 1991 & Rodriguez, 1999)**. The authors of history textbooks have been writing inaccurate facts about them for a long time (Salvucci, 1991 & Rodriguez, 1999). This is part of a combination of factors that has contributed to an unfriendly relationship between Mexico and the United States, which has caused this group of people to fail academically and be discriminated. For many teachers, what they read in textbooks is what they have to go by. Unfortunately, the information they read is not always accurate. <u>What teachers read affects how they view their Mexican-American students.</u> *Thesis Statement*

In a study by **Salvucci (1991),** the author compared the ten most popular history textbooks approved by the state of Texas. Texas is the state that has most influence on textbook sales in the United States. There is a public adoption hearing where parents and educators discuss what textbooks will be approved to educate the children. The authors of history textbooks not only have written them in a way that can make Americans perceive them as inferior, but these facts are inaccurate, and their presentation of the history is one sided. Salvucci (1991) divides her evaluation of the ten textbooks into four periods of history where she gives examples to show what information has been omitted, which makes it sound like a one-sided version of what really happened.

Textbook authors are under a great deal of pressure to include many things in a limited amount of pages. Even with this pressure, there is an omission of any reference to **Mexico and during the pre-Columbian era.** Some writers imply that "the history of the New World begins with the British, despite the fact that American Indians were the first to settle in what is now the United States" (**Salvucci, 1991, p. 206**). Also, the authors do not mention that the Aztec civilization, at its height, was comparable to the great societies of Europe" (p. 207). These examples give the impression that the pre-Columbian peoples had no major influence on the development of the Americas. Furthermore, they affect the Mexican-American students' self-esteem, which, in turn, affect their academic performances because they feel ambivalent between their culture and the United States' culture.

Almost all of the writers that Salvucci (1991) wrote about take an American viewpoint. According to Salvucci (1991), the textbook authors give a completely one-sided account of the **Texas Rebellion and the War** of 1847. For example, when one writer wrote about the Alamo, he did not even state that the Mexicans had the chance to surrender and the Texans viewed them as traitors. Here, the author is implying that the inferior people are the Mexicans. Moreover, he gives no account from the Mexican perspective. Another illustration is from the period of French intervention to the Mexican revolution. Another writer describes the events that happened during this period without mentioning the fact that five thousand Mexicans died while fighting the French. Also, "Benito Juárez, known as the Abraham Lincoln of Mexico," gets no mention either (p. 210). Again, one can see that no mention is made of either important people or what really happened during this period of history.

During World War I, World War II, the Korean War, and Vietnam, Mexicans were the work force of the United States of America. When the wars ended and they were no longer needed to maintain the work force in the United States, they were sent back to Mexico. They were called *braceros*. Most of the *braceros* were uneducated. This contributed to the stereotype that Mexicans are uneducated (Urrieta & Quach, 2000).

Also, the textbook writers put Mexican-Americans in the chapter that is about **minorities** when they refer to the recent past history. This chapter about minorities includes Blacks, Native American Indians, and the disabled (Salvucci, 1991). Also, the mention of Mexican-Americans such as San Antonio Mayor, Henry Cisneros, and Cesar Chávez, who have held positions with the United States government, helped Mexican-Americans and other Latinos fight for their rights, or made major contributions, receive few details about them. However, one thing they do talk a lot about is immigration. The recurring theme of giving little detail to the accomplishments and many details to the negative issues is carried out throughout all the periods of history (Salvucci, 1991 & Rodriguez, 1999).

Segregation of Mexican Americans is another topic that is not talked about in United States schools. Students are never taught the *Méndez vs. Westminster School District* case in 1945. The Civil Court of Appeals of Orange, California ruled that "Mexican-American **segregation** violated state laws and the

United States Constitution" (Rodriguez, 1999, p. 384). History books only write about *Brown vs. Board of Education*. The Méndez case occurred long before the *Brown vs. Board of Education*. Another instance where Mexican-Americans have been discriminated is with Propositions 187, 209, and 227. These propositions stated that, in California, "public institutions were not required to provide all Californians with the opportunity to succeed in education, economic security, and civil rights" (Rodriguez, 1999, p. 386). Mexican-Americans have always been discriminated and segregated since they have been in the United States; however, what is not written is how Mexican-Americans have been discriminated.

Whether the authors are writing about the accounts of battles or important people, they write it from an American perspective. They leave out important facts or just give few details. In essence, the writers create a negative image of the Mexican-Americans that American students read in textbooks. This teaches children that only American history is important and Mexican-American students get the message that their history is not important. As a result, Mexican-American students will have low self-esteem and the American education system has been effective in empowering them to reform to their way of thinking (Cummins, 1996 & Rodriguez, 1999).

So far, all that has been talked about is how Mexico, Mexicans, and Mexican-Americans are portrayed in books, and the message it carries. Another way that Mexican-Americans are viewed in the United States is by the **news media**. What needs to be understood is that it is very easy to believe what is said and written about different groups of people. Journalists write the way they do for a reason. The media relies on the meaning of language to convey its ideas and images (Vargas & dePyssler, 1998). The stories the media portray about Mexicans and Mexican-Americans to their readers and viewers are primarily of negative images. They include immigration and low academic achievement (Vargas & dePyssler, 1998). These inaccurate beliefs have led teachers to behave in pejorative ways toward their students who are not part of the majority (Barton & Osborne, 1995).

When one thinks of Mexicans, immigration is one of the first things that come to his mind. Of the all the minority groups in the United States, Mexicans are talked about the most regarding this topic. It is not hard for someone to conclude that, given the proximity between Mexico and the United States, crossing the border illegally would not be an uncommon occurrence. This has been portrayed in many movies (Vargas & dePyssler, 1998). Besides movies, immigration is also talked about in the news all the time (Salvucci, 1991; Vargas & dePyssler, 1998).

A big theme in the recent presidential election, and always a topic with any state, local, or federal government, is education, particularly low academic achievement among minority groups. A week doesn't go by without reading a news article in the paper or in a magazine regarding this issue. An article in the *New York Times* on October 22, 2000, stated that almost half of the students in the **bilingual education** or intensive English as a Second Language (ESL) classes failed to become fluent enough in English to move into mainstream classes. The same article questions whether bilingual or dual language programs really work (Steinberg, 2000). To further add to this topic, an editorial on November 8, 2000, in the *New York Times* states that fluency in more than one language is a good thing; however, the most important thing is being academically proficient in English. The editorial brings out both sides, although it favors neither one (Rothstein, 2000). It seems like the newspapers and magazines just talk about the negative aspects or quandaries on the recurring theme of bilingual education and multiculturalism, but never focuses on the actual problem and causes itself. The majority of the articles talk negatively about bilingualism and bilingual education.

The media has affected teachers' stereotypes toward minorities' education. All teachers, the general public, or children make the decision to believe what they read and hear. When they do not put these stereotypes aside, they will be biased. As a result, Mexican-Americans' academic performances will be affected.

References

Barton, Angela M., & Osborne, Margery D. (1995, April/May). Science for all
Americans? Science educational reform and Mexican-Americans. *The
High School Teacher, 78,* 244-52.

Cummins, Jim. (1996). *Negotiating identities: Education for empowerment in a
diverse society.* Ontario, CA: California Association for Bilingual Education.

Rodriguez, Alicia. (1999, Summer). Latino education, Latino movement. *Educational Theory, 49*(3), 381-400.

Rothstein, Richard. (2000, November 8). Bilingual ed: Debunking double talk.
The New York Times, p. A24.

Salvucci, Linda. (1991, February). Mexico, Mexicans, and Mexican-Americans in
secondary-school United States history books. *History Teacher, 24*(2),
203-22.

Steinberg, Jacques. (2000, October 22). Answers to an English question. Instead
of ending program, New York may offer a choice. *The New York Times*,
pp. B37, B40.

Urrieta, Luis Jr., & Quach, La Hue. (2000, October/November). My language
speaks of me: Transmutational identities in L2 acquisition. *The High
School Journal, 84*(1), 26-35.

Vargas, Lucila & dePyssler, Bruce. (1998, November/December). Using media
literacy to explore stereotypes of Mexican immigrants. *Social Education,
6*(7), 407-12.

Sample MLA Paper

Steven Jones

Professor Martinez

ESC 769

15 May 2001

History and the Portrayal of Mexican-Americans

History textbooks, books, journals, personal experiences, and magazines are the primary ways that children learn about their history and other groups' histories **(Salvucci 205)**. If one reads American history books and other books on Mexico, Mexicans, and Mexican-Americans, that person would possibly leave with a negative image of Mexico, Mexicans, and Mexican-Americans **(Rodriguez 390)**. The authors of history textbooks have been writing inaccurate facts about them for a long time (Salvucci 220). This is part of a combination of factors that has contributed to an unfriendly relationship between Mexico and the United States, which has caused this group of people to fail academically and be discriminated. For many teachers, what they read in textbooks is what they have to go by. Unfortunately, the information they read is not always accurate. <u>What teachers read affects how they view their Mexican-American students.</u>   *Thesis Statement*

In a study by Salvucci, the author compared the ten most popular history textbooks approved by the state of Texas. Texas is the state that has most influence on textbook sales in the United States. There is a public adoption hearing where parents and educators discuss what textbooks will be approved to educate the children. The authors of history textbooks not only have written them in a way that can make Americans perceive them as inferior, but these facts are inaccurate, and their presentation of the history is one sided. Salvucci divides her evaluation of the ten textbooks into four periods of history where she gives examples to show what information has been omitted, which makes it sound like a one-sided version of what really happened.

Textbook authors are under a great deal of pressure to include many things in a limited amount of pages. Even with this pressure, there is an omission of any reference to Mexico and during the pre-Columbian era. Some writers imply that "the history of the New World begins with the British, despite the fact that American Indians were the first to settle in what is now the United States" (Salvucci 206). Also, the authors do not mention that "the Aztec civilization, at its height, was comparable to the great societies of Europe" **(207)**. These examples give the impression that the pre-Columbian peoples had no major influence on the development of the Americas. Furthermore, they affect the Mexican-American students' self-esteem, which, in turn, affect their academic performances because they feel ambivalent between their culture and the United States' culture.

Almost all of the writers that Salvucci wrote about take an American viewpoint. According to Salvucci, the textbook authors give a completely one-sided account of the Texas Rebellion and the War of 1847. For example, when one writer wrote about the Alamo, he did not even state that the Mexicans had the chance to surrender and the Texans viewed them as traitors. Here, the author is implying that the inferior people are the Mexicans. Moreover, he gives no account from the Mexican perspective (209). Another illustration is from the period of French intervention to the

Jones 3

to the Mexican revolution. Another writer describes the events that happened during this period without mentioning the fact that five thousand Mexicans died while fighting the French. Also, "Benito Juárez, known as the Abraham Lincoln of Mexico," gets no mention either (210). Again, one can see that no mention is made of either important people or what really happened during this period of history.

During World War I, World War II, the Korean War, and Vietnam, Mexicans were the work force of the United States of America. When the wars ended and they were no longer needed to maintain the work force in the United States, they were sent back to Mexico. They were called *braceros*. Most of the *braceros* were uneducated. This contributed to the stereotype that Mexicans are uneducated (Urrieta & Quach 30).

Also, the textbook writers put Mexican-Americans in the chapter that is about minorities when they refer to the recent past history. This chapter about minorities includes Blacks, Native American Indians, and the disabled (Salvucci 211). Also, the mention of Mexican-Americans such as San Antonio Mayor, Henry Cisneros, and Cesar Chávez (211-212), who have held positions with the United States government, helped Mexican-Americans and other Latinos fight for their rights, or made major contributions, receive few details about them. However, one thing they do talk a lot about is immigration. The recurring theme of giving little detail to the accomplishments and many details to the negative issues is carried out throughout all the periods of history (Rodriguez 387).

Segregation of Mexican Americans is another topic that is not talked about in

United States schools. Students are never taught the *Méndez vs. Westminster School District* case in 1945. The Civil Court of Appeals of Orange County, California, ruled that "Mexican-American segregation violated state laws and the United States Constitution" (Rodriguez 384). History books only write about *Brown vs. Board of Education.* The Méndez case occurred long before the *Brown vs. Board of Education.* Another instance where Mexican-Americans have been discriminated is with Propositions 187, 209, and 227. These propositions stated that, in California, "public institutions were not required to provide all Californians with the opportunity to succeed in education, economic security, and civil rights" (Rodriguez 386). Mexican-Americans have always been discriminated and segregated since they have been in the United States; however, what is not written is how Mexican-Americans have been discriminated.

Whether the authors are writing about the accounts of battles or important people, they write it from an American perspective. They leave out important facts or just give few details. In essence, the writers create a negative image of the Mexican-Americans that American students read in textbooks. This teaches children that only American history is important and Mexican-American students get the message that their history is not important
As a result, Mexican-American students will have low self-esteem and the American education system has been effective in empowering them to reform to their way of thinking (Cummins 56).

So far, all that has been talked about is how Mexico, Mexicans, and Mexican-Americans are portrayed in books, and the message it carries. Another way that

Jones 5

Mexican-Americans are viewed in the United States is by the news media. What needs to be understood is that it is very easy to believe what is said and written about different groups of people. Journalists write the way they do for a reason. The media relies on the meaning of language to convey its ideas and images (Vargas & dePyssler 410). The stories the media portray about Mexicans and Mexican-Americans to their readers and viewers are primarily of negative images. They include immigration and low academic achievement **(Vargas & dePyssler 407)**. These inaccurate beliefs have led teachers to behave in pejorative ways toward their students who are not part of the majority (Barton & Osborne 245).

When one thinks of Mexicans, immigration is one of the first things that come to his mind. Of the all the minority groups in the United States, Mexicans are talked about the most regarding this topic. It is not hard for someone to conclude that, given the proximity between Mexico and the United States, crossing the border illegally would not be an uncommon occurrence. This has been portrayed in many movies (Vargas & dePyssler 410). Besides movies, immigration is also talked about in the news all the time (Vargas & dePyssler 411).

A big theme in the recent presidential election, and always a topic with any state, local, or federal government, is education, particularly low academic achievement among minority groups. A week doesn't go by without reading a news article in the paper or in a magazine regarding this issue. An article in the *New York Times* on October 22, 2000, stated that almost half of the students in the bilingual education or intensive English as a Second Language (ESL) classes failed to become fluent enough in English to move into mainstream classes. The same article questions whether bilingual or dual language programs really work (Steinberg B40). To further add to this topic, an editorial on November 8, 2000, in the *New York Times* states that fluency in more than one language is a good thing; however, the most important thing is being academically proficient in English. The editorial brings out both sides, although it favors neither one (Rothstein A24). It seems like the newspapers and magazines just talk about the negative aspects or quandaries on the recurring theme of bilingual education and multiculturalism, but never focuses on the actual problem and causes itself. The majority of the articles talk negatively about bilingualism and bilingual education.

The media has affected teachers' stereotypes toward minorities' education. All teachers, the general public, or children make the decision to believe what they read and hear. When they do not put these stereotypes aside, they will be biased. As a result, Mexican-Americans' academic performances will be affected.

History textbooks, books, journals, personal experiences, and magazines are the primary ways that children learn about their history and other groups' histories (Salvucci, 1991 & Rodriguez, 1999). If one reads American history books and other books on Mexico, Mexicans, and Mexican-Americans, that person would possibly leave with a negative image of Mexico, Mexicans, and Mexican-Americans **(Salvucci, 1991 & Rodriguez, 1999)**. The authors of history textbooks have been writing inaccurate facts about them for a long time (Salvucci, 1991 & Rodriguez, 1999). This is part of a combination of factors that has contributed to an unfriendly relationship between Mexico and the United States, which has caused this group of people to fail academically and be discriminated. For many teachers, what they read in textbooks is what they have to go by. Unfortunately, the information they read is not always accurate. <u>What teachers read affects how they view their Mexican-American students.</u> *Thesis Statement*

In a study by **<u>Salvucci (1991)</u>,** the author compared the ten most popular history textbooks approved by the state of Texas. Texas is the state that has most influence on textbook sales in the United States. There is a public adoption hearing where parents and educators discuss what textbooks will be approved to educate the children. The authors of history textbooks not only have written them in a way that can make Americans perceive them as inferior, but these facts are inaccurate, and their presentation of the history is one sided. Salvucci (1991) divides her evaluation of the ten textbooks into four periods of history where she gives examples to show what information has been omitted, which makes it sound like a one-sided version of what really happened.

Works Cited

Barton, Angela M., & Osborne, Margery D. "Science for all Americans? Science educational reform and Mexican-Americans." The High School Teacher 78, (1995): 244-52.

Cummins, Jim. Negotiating identities: Education for empowerment in a diverse society. Ontario, CA: California Association for Bilingual Education, 1996.

Rodriguez, Alicia. "Latino education, Latino movement." Educational Theory 49, (1999): 381-400.

Rothstein, Richard. "Bilingual ed: Debunking double talk." The New York Times 8 November 2000: A24.

Salvucci, Linda. "Mexico, Mexicans, and Mexican-Americans in secondary-school United States history books." History Teacher 24.2 (1991): 203-22.

Steinberg, Jacques. "Answers to an English question. Instead of ending program, New York may offer a choice." The New York Times 22 October 2000: B37, B40.

Urrieta, Luis Jr., & Quach, La Hue. "My language speaks of me: Transmutational identities in L2 acquisition." The High School Journal 84.1 (2000): 26-35.

Vargas, Lucila & dePyssler, Bruce. "Using media literacy to explore stereotypes of Mexican immigrants." Social Education 6.7 (1998): 407-12.

Chapter 5

Proposals and Presentations

A *proposal* is, as its name says, a type of essay whose purpose is to persuade the acceptance of an idea. There are different types of proposals. There are different types of proposals depending on the purpose and nature of the topic. In proposals that involve human subjects, as in the sample proposal in this chapter, the investigators need to get permission from the National Institute of Health (NIH) first. Also, each researcher needs to take an online test that will certify him or her to conduct research on human subjects. The majority of the proposal's sections (i.e., methods, results, risk of injury to participants, and confidentiality and anonymity) need to be written in future tense because the study has yet not been executed. Let us look at the following components of a proposal more closely:

a. **Executive Summary.** This is the literature review of a proposal.

b. **Methods.** This section discusses the selection of the subjects, the procedures for the study, and the analysis of the results.

c. **Ethical considerations.** This means that the researcher(s) have to protect the subjects' welfare and identity at all times.

d. **Risk of Injury to Participants.** This part is especially important to

studies that involve drug testing or medical issues. The researcher(s) must
state what harm, if any, can be inflicted to the subjects during the course
of the study.

e. **Confidentiality and Anonymity.** The names of subjects of the study can
not be stated for any reasons. Codes or initials must be used. The participants must also know that they may abort the study at any time by telling
the investigator(s) in writing.

f. **Limitations and Biases.** The faults of the study and what cannot be accounted for are discussed here. The investigator(s) must also state how the
results can be invalid and not reliable.

g. **Financial Budget.** If necessary, the researcher(s) can ask for financial
assistance. They must prepare a budget and attach it along with the consent
forms and any questionnaires.

Sample Proposal

The Understanding of Academic English between Native and

Non-Native Speakers

By

John Doe

Abstract

This study compares the comprehension of oral academic discourse by monolingual, English as a Second Language (ESL), and bilingual college students. The
students took notes in a naturalistic environment in their actual classes. There
are four groups: (a) ESL students; (b) monolingual English; (c) bilingual students, whose first language (L1) is English; and (d) bilingual students, whose
second language (L2) is English. Their notes were collected and analyzed for
linguistic and content errors. The results are expected to suggest that the students in this study take poor notes and they leave out some of the most important information.

Executive Summary

Lectures are the principal way that students clarify academic facts in college. All college students know that taking notes while listening to a lecture is very difficult. The student must do many things at the same time to understand lectures. However, students must master this complex form of academic discourse in order to do well in college.

Academic discourse comprises many things. One is to comprehend the lecture. Another component is the pragmatics and the actual discourse of lectures. This includes lecture styles and lexico-grammatical features (Flowerdew, 1994a). In order to understand what is going on in class, one must understand the professors' utterances, which means one must understand the speech of the person speaking. This is called *auditory comprehension* (Nicolosi, Harryman, & Kresheck, 1996).

In order to understand a lecture, students must go through a series of steps: (a) listen; (b) pick out pertinent information; (c) summarize the information; (d) write it down (Fahmy, Jackson, & Bilton, 1990; Johnson, 1992; Kangli, 1995; Kiewra, K., Mayer, R., Christensen, M., Kim, S., & Risch, N., 1991a; Lively, Pisoni, van Summers, & Bernacki, 1993; Parks, 1982; Reed, 2000; Scerbo et al, 1992; Sitler, 1997; Tauroza, 2001). Some professors speak for long periods of time, which does not give students enough time to take notes (Koren, 1997). Also, the rate at which the professors speak can affect the ability of students to comprehend what they are saying (Burke & Wyatt-Smith, 1996; Fahmy, Jackson, & Bilton, 1990). Many factors are crucial for students to understand academic discourse and take notes simultaneously.

Students may have problems understanding lectures for several reasons. One reason may be that they are not familiar with the lecture format (Tauroza & Allison, 1994). Fahmay, Jackson, and Bilton (1990) describe the three main styles of lectures professors give. Another way of delivering a lecture is presented by Sitler (1997). Sitler proposed a way to teach students and to give them a chance to take notes by building in time into the lecture just for this purpose. However, there are disadvantages to this method such as how much material that can be covered during a class.

Another problem may be that the student does not understand the professor's accent because he or she has not been exposed to it before (Flowerdew, 1994b; Major, Fitzmaurice, Bunta, & Balasubramanian, 2002). Surveys have been done to illustrate the importance that accents have on auditory comprehension during lectures (Burke & Wyatt-Smith, 1996). Intonational cues may also cause misunderstandings (Selkirk, 1995). The English language may cause problems for English language learners (ELLs). If ELLs are not proficient in English or they are not familiar with certain lecture styles, they may fail to get the full meaning of the lecture; therefore, they may not do well in the class (Burke and Wyatt-Smith, 1996). Finally, cultural issues may cause problems for all students, especially ELLs.

Many studies have been completed on note-taking. They have discussed how to use notes to attain better studying skills and to improve the quality of notes. Other studies have focused on recalling information for tests (Kangli, 1995; Kiewra et al., 1995, 1999). However, few studies have specifically investigated the linguistic aspects of note-taking during a college lecture. Kiewra and his colleagues (1991a, 1991b; 1995), along with other researchers, used a laboratory setting for all their experiments. Their studies concentrated around the functions of note-taking and the recalling of information. The problem with these studies is that when the students take notes, they know that they are being tested. In addition, their notes may be different from when they take notes during their regular lecture classes (Locke, 1977; Tauroza, 2001).

However, few studies are done in naturalistic environments (Chaudron 1983; Clerehan, 1995; Kelly, 1997; King, 1994; Koren, 1997; McKenna, 1987; Murphy & Candlin, 1979). Studying what students do during real lectures makes their note-taking more authentic. For example, Koren (1997) studied students taking a law class in an Israeli university to see if they translate their notes into their native languages. Another investigation done by King (1994) looks at the quantity of four English language learners' notes in regards to the visual and verbal messages. Few studies focus on the linguistic aspects of the students' notes. The present study looks at the linguistic content of notes taken by English as a Second Language students, monolingual students, and bilingual students to determine if they have successfully understood their class lectures.

The purpose of this study is to compare comprehension of oral academic discourse by monolingual English, English as a Second Language (ESL), and bilingual students. The research question for this study is: What is the relationship between the content of a lecture (what the professor said) and the content of the notes taken by English as a Second Language, monolingual and bilingual students?

Methods

Subjects. Four groups of undergraduate and prospective college students were studied. An ESL American College Testing (ACT) writing workshop comprised nine Hispanic students; two were male and seven were female. An undergraduate experimental psychology class contained the other three groups. One group was made up of eight female monolingual English students. Another group consisted of three female bilingual students, whose L1 is English. Their second languages were Spanish, French, and Creole. The last group of six female and one male bilingual students whose L2 is English had mother tongues of Greek, Spanish, and Korean.

Procedures. In both classes, their professors will only speak. None of them will write anything on the blackboard or hand out any papers. The students will be asked to take notes on a one-hour lecture as they normally do on a topic in accordance to their syllabi. Once the lecture is over, the investigator will Xerox their notes and return it to them the next day.

The class notes will be analyzed for their content about the lecture. They will be analyzed by two other people as well as the investigator. Careful attention will be used when looking at the many possible formats for class notes. For validity and reliability, the results of this study will be compared to the results of previous studies.

Ethical Considerations

Risk of Injury to Participants. There will be minimal or no risk to the subjects' health during this study.

Confidentiality and Anonymity. The subjects will have to sign a consent form allowing them to participate in this experiment. Their names will not be mentioned. Instead, they will be given a code name or a name of their choosing. In addition to anonymity, all information about the participants will be kept confidential. Only the investigators will have access to this information.

Limitations and Biases

This study is limited to the two college classes as intact groups. Due to the nature of the study, many professors would not let the investigator use their classes. Thus, the number of participants and classes is not as many as hoped for.

References

Burke, E. & Wyatt-Smith, C. (1996, March). Academic and nonacademic diffi-

culties: Perceptions of graduate non-English speaking background stu-

dents. *TESL-EJ*, 2 (1). Retrieved March 2002, from

http://www-writing.berkeley.edu/TESL-EJ/ej05/a1.html.

Chaudron, C. (1983). Simplification of input: Topic reinstatements and their ef-

fects on L2 learners' recognition and recall. *TESOL Quarterly*, 17 (3),

437-458.

Clerehan, R. (1995). Taking it down: Note-taking practices of L1 and L2 stu-

dents. *English for Specific Purposes*, 14 (2), 137-155. Retrieved Octo-

ber 15, 2001, from

http://www.sciencedirect.com/science/journal/08894906.

Fahmy, J., & Bilton, L. (1990). *Lecture comprehension and note-taking for L2
students*. (ERIC Document Reproductive Service No. ED323785)

Flowerdew, J. (1994a). *Academic Listening: Research Perspectives*. Cambridge,

UK: Cambridge University Press.

Flowerdew, J. & Peacock, M. (2001). *Research Perspectives on English for Aca-

demic Purposes*. Cambridge, UK: Cambridge University Press.

Johnson, J. (1992). Critical Period Effects in Second Language Acquisition: The

Effect of Written vs. Auditory Materials on the Assessment of Gram-

matical Competence. *Language Learning*, 42 (4), 217-248.

Kangli, J. (1995, July). *Cohesion, script, and note-taking in consecutive interpreta-tion.* (ERIC Document Reproductive Service No. ED398726)

Kelly, R. (1977). Monologue discourse in situ: an analysis of the paralinguistic and extralinguistic aspects of an engineering lecture. Unpublished master's thesis, University of Lancaster.

Kiewra, K., Dubois, N., Christian, D., McShane, A., Meyerhoffer, M., & Roskelley, D. (1991a, June). Note-taking functions and techniques. *Journal of Educational Psychology*, 83 (2), 240-245.

Kiewra, K., Mayer, R., Christensen, M., Kim, S., & Risch, N. (1991b, March). Effects of repetition on recall and note-taking: Strategies for learning from lectures. *Journal of Educational Psychology*, 83 (1), 120-124.

Kiewra, K. et al. (1995, April). Effects of note-taking format and study technique on recall and relational performance. *Contemporary Educational Psychology*, 20 (2), 172-187.

King, P. (1994). Visual and verbal messages in the engineering lecture: Note-taking by postgraduate L2 students. In John Flowerdew (Ed.), *Academic Listening: Research Perspectives* (pp. 219-238). Cambridge, UK: Cambridge University Press.

Koren, S. (1997, June). Listening to lectures in L2: Taking notes in L1. *TESL-EJ*, 2(4). Retrieved September 18, 2001, from the World Wide Web: http://www-writing.berkeley.edu/TESL-EJ/ej08/a1.html.

Lively, S., Pisoni, D., van Summers, W., & Bernacki, R. (1993, May/June). Effects of cognitive workload on speech production: Acoustic analyses and perceptual consequences. *Journal of the Acoustic Society of America*, 93 (5), 2962-2973.

Locke, E. (1977, November/December). An empirical study of lecture notetaking among college students. *Journal of Educational Research*, 71 (2), 93-99.

Major, R., Fitzmaurice, S., Bunta, F., & Balasubramanian, C. (2002, Summer). The effects of nonnative accents on listening comprehension: Implications for ESL assessment. *TESOL Quarterly*, 36 (2), 173-190.

McKenna, E. (1987). Preparing foreign students to enter discourse communities. *English for Specific Purposes*, 6, 187-202.

Murphy, D. & Candlin, C. (1979). Engineering lecture discourse and listening comprehension. Practical Papers in English Language Education, Vol. 2. UK: University of Lancaster.

Nicolosi, L., Harryman, E., & Kresheck, J. (1996). Terminology of Communication Disorders: Speech-Language-Hearing (4th ed). Baltimore, Maryland: Williams & Wilkins, 69.

Parks, G. (1982). Notes on the use of translation in language classes. *System*, 10 (3), 241-245.

Reed, M. (2000). He who hesitates: Hesitation phenomena as a quality control in speech production, obstacles, in non-native speech perception. *Journal of Education*, 182 (3), 67-91.

Scerbo, M., Warm, J., Dember, W., & Grasha, A. (1992, October). Role of time and cuing in a college lecture. *Contemporary Educational Psychology*, 17 (4), 312-328.

Sitler, H. (1997, Summer). The spaced lecture. *College Teaching*, 45 (3), 108-110.

Tauroza, S. (2001). Second language lecture comprehension research in naturalistic controlled conditions. In John Flowerdew and Mathew Peacock (Eds.), *Research Perspectives on English for Academic Purposes* (pp. 360-374). Cambridge, UK: Cambridge University Press.

Tauroza, S. & Allison, D. (1994). Expectation-driven understanding in information systems lecture comprehension. In John Flowerdew (Ed.), *Academic Listening: Research Perspectives* (pp. 35-54). Cambridge, UK: Cambridge University Press.

Appendices

English Consent Form

Lehman College THE CITY UNIVERSITY OF
NEW YORK
Division of Education   **Department of Middle**
and High School Education

250 Bedford Park Blvd. West   Shuster 120
Bronx, N.Y. 33333

Investigator:	Institutional Contact:
John Doe	Joan Smith
122-68 Booth Avenue	Assistant Director
Bayside, NY 11368	Carmen Hall, 120
(718) 567-5555	Lehman College/CUNY
JohnDoe@hotmail.com	Bronx, NY 33333
	(718) 456-7777

Study Description:

You have been invited to participate in a study by Mr. John Doe that tests Hispanic college students' understanding of spoken English during a college lecture. Mr. Doe is a graduate student here at Lehman College. You were selected because you are a Hispanic college student. If you choose to be in the study, Mr. Doe will meet with you once in a classroom. He will ask you to take notes during a college lecture, and you can choose to leave the lecture at any time. Mr. Doe will record the lecture to make it easier for him to write down what the professor said. The lecture will take about 60 minutes. If you agree participate, please sign below and return the form to Mr. Doe.

Your Rights, Privacy and Welfare:

1. Mr. Doe will report what you and others have written during the lecture. However, Mr. Bookman will never mention you by name. You can choose a code name for yourself, or he will identify you by a letter. No one will have access to the videotape, but Mr. Doe and his adviser. After the study, he will destroy the tapes.

2. You are free not to participate. You are also free to stop being in the study at any time. You do not have to answer any questions that you don't want to answer. This will not affect you, your grades, or your academic record in any way.

3. If you have questions or concerns about this study or your rights as a participant, please contact Mr. Doe or Ms. Banks at the telephone numbers above.

I have read this consent form, and I understand the procedures to be used in this study. I freely and voluntarily choose to be in Mr. Bookman's study. I understand that I can stop being in the study at any time without penalty.

Name (please print):

_____

Signature:_____

Date:_____

English Screening Form

The purpose of this study is to investigate how well Latino college students understand spoken English. You will be asked to listen to a college lecture and take notes on it. Your comprehension of the college lecture is going to be evaluated by the quality of your notes. This form is to verify you meet the requirements to be a participant in this study. All of the information on this page will be kept confidential.

Name _____   Today's date _____

Sex: Male   Female
Occupation _____   Referred by _____
Telephone _____   Age _____
Birth date _____   Place of birth _____

At what age did you learn English? _____

Other languages you speak:
Comprehension _____
Oral_____
Written _____

Interviewer's impression of dominance in English:
_____
_____
_____

	Self-evaluation			
Scale	Okay	Very good	Well	Excellent
	1	2	3	4

English:

Comprehension _____

Oral _____

Written_____

Average _____

Dominate language _____

Signature of participant _____

Spanish:

Comprehension_____

Oral _____

Written _____

Average _____

Date _____

Presentations

Presentations are common in-class assignments. A presentation is when someone presents a topic to a group of people. This is not a favorite assignment for
most students. If a student is shy or has a fear of speaking in front of a group of
people, he or she has to get used to it. There are ways to get over this fear of
speaking in front of a classroom.

Most of the time, students are expected to present a specific topic discussed
in class to their classmates. They usually have a piece of paper with an outline
of their presentations. This is very stressful for most students because their
peers, as well as their professors, are judging them in the classroom. If it is a
speech at a professional conference, then professionals are judging the presenter.
Regardless, this situation makes anyone nervous because everyone wants to be
accepted by his or her peers or colleagues. Any speech can be less worrisome if
it is broken down into three steps: (1) planning; (2) practicing; and (3) presenting.

Planning

When giving a speech, it must be organized, so it follows a logical order. It
must catch the audience's attention from the start. Then, it has to be organized
in a logical manner, including a conclusion. Finally, the last part is a short question and answer period.

Catching the audience's attention is the most important part of the speech.
The very beginning of a presentation determines if the audience is interested in
it. If the audience is not interested from the start, they might not pay attention to
the presenter. In a classroom, this could mean that the professor will get a negative impression about the rest of the presentation; he or she may be looking for
anything negative at this point. At a professional conference, the audience will
look for another presentation. This could look bad for the presenter for future
publications and presentations at conferences. Hence, it is very important to
capture the audience's attention immediately.

Catching the audience's attention can be done in two ways. One way is to
ask the people listening to the presenter a question that will get them engaged in
the topic. Another way is to start with a situation or scenario that will bring the
audience into the topic of the presentation.

The logical order of a presentation is also part of the organization. The struc-
ture of a speech is like an essay. It must have an introduction, body, and conclusion. Part of the introduction is catching the audience's attention. The other
part to the introduction is to briefly discuss the purpose of the presentation.
Sometimes, presenters even give a brief outline of how it will be organized.

The body of the presentation is the support and explanation of the purpose.
During a speech, one cannot talk about all the details or results because of the

limited time given. Thus, the speaker must summarize what are the most important points. Videos, results of experiments, and facts can be used to do explain the details.

Conclusions are more than just summaries. The conclusion of the presentation must tie together how the information in the body is related to the purpose. The presenter must restate the purpose of the presentation, and the most important facts or findings. Future research or opinions are recommended if the speech is about a scientific topic. Therefore, it may be easier to think of a presentation like an essay or scientific article.

Finally, there is a question and answer period in which the presenter answers any questions the audience has. During this part of the presentation, the presenter must be prepared to answer any questions. In some cases, the questions cannot be answered because research has not addressed that particular topic. Regardless, all questions must be answered. The presenter should never fake an answer. If he or she does not know, the response can be in reference to future research.

Practicing

Once the planning is completed, it must be practiced. It is not recommended to present without practicing. The time allotted for a presentation goes by fast. Recording oneself and playing it back reveals what needs to be adjusted. Therefore, it is crucial that the presenter knows how much time it takes to discuss each segment. Also, the speech rate is very important. Many times, nervous presenters speak very fast. The speech rate should be moderate, yet slow enough, for the audience to digest the information.

Practicing can be done by rehearsing in front of a mirror. Many students will laugh at themselves when they do this. This suggests that they are not ready to give their speeches. When they do not laugh, they are ready to give their presentations. Rehearsing in front a mirror allows the presenter to see his or her nonverbal communication such as body posture and hand movements. These things can distract the audience. Another way to rehearse is by practicing in front of a group of friends.

Presenting

The presenter is going to be nervous in many cases the day of the presentation. He or she should keep a checklist of things such as nonverbal communication that needs to be followed. For example, body posture is very important. A tall, erect body posture is necessary. Anything else signifies that the presenter is not professional or serious unless it is done to prove a point.

It is also recommended that the presenter does not read from a piece of paper. He or she must look at the audience. Lack of eye contact can mean to the audience that the presenter is not thoroughly prepared. An easy way to do this is to look at three people in the audience who are all in the middle row: far right, dead center, and far left. Everyone will think the person presenting is looking at him or her.

Having a loud voice is helpful when giving presentations. If the presenter does not have a loud voice, then he or she can request a microphone. The presenter cannot be effective if the audience cannot hear what he or she is saying. Therefore, the audience cannot follow the presentation easily.

To recap, there are many things that must happen before the day of the presentation. No presentation can be effective and good if the presenter is not ready to present or does not capture the audience's attention quickly. Thus, it is important to understand and know what exactly is going to be said during the presentation.

BIBLIOGRAPHY

Douglas Lind, William Marchal, and Samuel Wathen. *Statistical Techniques in Business and Economics*, New York: MacGraw Hill, 2005.

Fahmay, J. and Bilton, L. *Lecture Comprehension and Note-Taking for L2 Students*, 1990. (ERIC Document Reproductive Service No. ED323785)

Goldsmith, J. *The Handout of Phonological Theory*, Cambridge, MA: Blackwell, 1995.

Gujarati, Damodar. *Basic Econometrics*, New York: MacGraw Hill, 2003.

Johnston, Jack and John Dinardo. *Econometric Methods*, New York: MacGraw Hill, 1997.

Koren, S. Listening to Lectures in L2: Taking Notes in L1. *TESL-EJ*, 2(4). Retrieved September 18, 2004, from the World Wide Web: http://www-writing.berkerly.edu/TESL-EJ/ej08/a1.html, 1997.

Larson, Ron and Betsy Farber. *Elementary Statistics*. New Jersey: Prentice Hall. 2000.

Lively, S., Pisoni, D., van Summers, W., and Bernacki, R. Effects of Cognitive Workload on Speech Production. *Journal of the Acoustic society of America*, 1993, 93(5), 2962-2973.

Salvatore, Dominick. *Statistics and Econometrics*, New York: MacGraw Hill, 1982.

Scerbo, M., Warm, J., Dember, W., and Grasha, A. Role of Time and Cueing in a College Lecture. *Contemporary Educational Psychology*, 1992, 17(4), 312-328.

Selkirk, E. Sentence prosody: Intonation, stress, and phrasing. In J. Selkirk (Ed.), The Handbook of Phonological Theory, Cambridge, MA: Blackwell, 1995.

Studenmund, A. H. *Using Econometrics*, Boston: Addison Wesley Longman, 1970.

— *Eviews 5*, Irvine: Quantitative Micro Software, 2004

Warburton, Christopher. *Research and Profit Maximization in Finance and Economics*, Maryland: University Press of America, 2006.

INDEX